Television as a Cultural Force

Richard Adler   Project Editor,
TV Workshop

Douglass Cater   Editor, Aspen Series on
Communications and Society

Published with the
Aspen Institute Program on
Communications and Society

**The Praeger Special Studies program—utiliz-
ing the most modern and efficient book production techniques and a selective worldwide
distribution network—makes available to the
academic, government, and business communities significant, timely research in U.S. and
international economic, social, and political
development.**

Television as a Cultural Force

PRAEGER SPECIAL STUDIES IN U.S. ECONOMIC, SOCIAL, AND POLITICAL ISSUES

Praeger Publishers New York Washington London

Library of Congress Cataloging in Publication Data

Main entry under title:

Television as a cultural force.

(Praeger special studies in U.S. economic, social, and
political issues)
Bibliography: p. 175
1. Television programs—United States—Addresses,
essays, lectures.   2. Television criticism—Addresses,
essays, lectures.   I. Adler, Richard, 1942-   II. Cater,
Douglass, 1923-
PN1992.3.U5T38   791.45'09   76-10714
ISBN 0-275-23180-1 (cloth)
ISBN 0-915436-19-1 (paper)

PRAEGER PUBLISHERS
111 Fourth Avenue, New York, N.Y. 10003, U.S.A.

Published in the United States of America in 1976
by Praeger Publishers, Inc.

© 1976 by the Aspen Institute Program on Communications & Society
Printed in the United States of America
Book composition by Diane Willis and Curt Chelin

Preface

A primary interest of the Aspen Institute Program on Communications and Society has been television's effects on our life and our culture. As TV approached its twenty-fifth anniversary as a household phenomenon, the Program in 1974 established a Workshop devoted to this interest. Our goal has been to persuade outstanding humanists, scholars, and critics to give more attention to the role of television in society. *Television as a Social Force*, an earlier volume published last year, represented the first results of this involvement. Now, *Television as a Cultural Force* is the sequel.

The two books are intended as ventures in the field of television criticism. We hope that others will follow with the increasing recognition of TV's impact on the lives of individuals and of the nation. The Aspen Workshop has plans for a handbook on "How to Watch Prime Time TV." This has become an essential skill.

We wish to express our appreciation to the National Endowment for the Humanities and the John & Mary Markle Foundation, which have provided support for the Workshop on Television.

—Douglass Cater

Table of Contents

Introduction:
A Context for Criticism

Richard Adler

Perhaps with television, more than with other popular
arts, there has been confusion as to purpose and definition. No one seems to know just what the medium
is . . .

—Horace Newcomb

This volume is the second collection of essays to come from
the Aspen Program's Workshop on Television. The Workshop was
established in 1974 to stimulate fresh assessments of TV's impact
on society and to focus attention on the role of this pervasive
medium. *Television as a Social Force*, published in 1975, was the
first product of the Workshop. It contained eight original essays
examining the significance of the first twenty-five years of television in America. Specific subjects included the impact of the
medium on our attitudes toward ourselves and the world, a comparison of television journalism and print journalism, a study of the
influence of TV news on political legitimacy, and a look at the

Mr. Adler is Assistant Director of the Aspen Institute Program on
Communications and Society and is Director of its Workshop on
Television. He is also serving as a Research Associate at the Harvard
Graduate School of Education.

medium's future.

During the past year, the Workshop has moved from general consideration of the medium's role in society to intensive examination of specific television programs and genres. A series of six meetings were held: two in California, two in New York, one in Chicago, and a final conference in Aspen during July 1975. Participants included scholars from a variety of disciplines, working television critics, and professionals from the television industry. At each meeting, participants viewed specific programs, then tried to practice the best sort of criticism possible. Since television is rarely viewed in this way, these occasions for discourse and controversy were invaluable. The discussions also revealed that a number of current prime-time programs were of sufficient aesthetic and thematic interest to withstand sustained critical scrutiny. These essays are the results of this process.

The starting premise of this book is that television has not received the kind of criticism it deserves. Television has become the primary source of news and entertainment for most Americans; yet it is ignored as a subject of serious criticism. By serious criticism, I mean the informed response and analysis that exists in abundance for literature, film, drama, and the other performing arts.

A number of explanations have been offered as to why television has failed to receive serious critical attention:

The medium is so new and has grown so quickly there has not been time to develop critical approaches . . .

Television is a "cultural wasteland," unworthy of serious attention . . .

Television is not an art form at all, but merely a business whose purpose is to sell audiences to advertisers . . .

The contents of television programming are not the expressions of identifiable individuals, but corporate creations . . .

There is so much television that no critic can hope to (or want to) follow closely the development of the medium.

Some of these assertions are undoubtedly true; others are open to challenge. For example, the argument based on the newness of the medium grows less convincing as television passes its twenty-fifth anniversary. And, while it is indisputable that television is a business, it is not at all clear why this is necessarily antithetical to a consideration of the medium as an art form. Television in this country *does* derive its revenues from sponsors, not viewers. But it is still the viewing audience which chooses what it will watch and, thus, has the power to determine what will succeed or fail.

A more basic reason for the current state of television criticism, I believe, is the mass nature of the medium. If television is an art form, it is surely the most popular of the arts. As such, attitudes toward television have been shaped by a larger controversy over the significance and value of popular culture—a controversy which predates the advent of television. There has always been a traditional bias against works of popular culture by critics and intellectuals who hold that popular culture can only be of interest as sociological phenomena. (Interestingly, social scientists have treated television with considerable seriousness since its inception: a recent compilation lists more than 2,300 separate items of "scientific literature" concerned with "television and human behavior."[1])

The problem with this cultural bias is that it is inimical to the spirit of enlightened criticism. It precludes the possibility of judging television content on its own merits, simply because the material appears on television. If this country has a unifying culture, it is the mass, popular culture; and today, television is the most vital expression of that culture. We need television criticism which is neither simplistic nor patronizing, criticism which will provide both a language for describing what appears on the screen and standards for discriminating excellence from mediocrity.

Horace Newcomb suggests that another barrier to better television criticism is television's peculiar nature, which creates persistent "confusion as to [its] purpose and definition."[2] It is true that television has borrowed generously from other, older media. Television is, nevertheless, more than the sum of its antecedents. It has a number of characteristics which make it unique and which provide a special challenge to the critic. I would like to discuss four of these characteristics, as a context for the essays which follow.

Diversity

One of the most familiar charges against American television is that it is a "vast cultural wasteland."[3] The phrase suggests a monotonous, undifferentiated landscape devoid of interest or life. The metaphor was overstated when first applied, and it is even less appropriate today. Whatever flaws television has, a lack of variety is not one of them. Consider, for example, the selection of programs that were available in the San Francisco Bay Area at 9 p.m. on Sunday, January 4, 1976:[4]

Channel and Affiliation	Program
2 — Independent	Conclusion of a live broadcast of a professional basketball game, followed by a film on the threat to wildlife posed by pollution in the San Francisco Bay.
4 — NBC	"McCoy" — Tony Curtis as a private eye.
5 — CBS	"Kojak" — Telly Savalas as a streetwise New York City homocide detective.
7 — ABC	"ABC Theater" — *Collision Course*, a two-hour re-enactment of the confrontation between President Truman and General MacArthur over the conduct of the Korean War, with E. G. Marshall and Henry Fonda.
9 — PBS	"Masterpiece Theater" — The first of 13 new installments of the third season of "Upstairs, Downstairs"— concerns the impact of World War I on this now-familiar English household.

20 — Independent	Locally oriented Japanese language discussion program.
36 — Independent	"Don Kirshner's Rock Concert" — Performances by the Nitty Gritty Dirt Band and Kool and the Gang.
38 — Independent	"Mr. Gospel Guitar"
44 — Independent	"Lou Gordon" — Discussion program, with the author of a book on breast cancer and the man who helped Jimmy Hoffa write his autobiography.
54 — PBS	A 2½-hour re-enactment of the Watergate cover-up trial.

One might note that, on this varied menu, one category unrepresented is the fine arts. But one hour later, Channel 9, the public television station, offered "Music From Aspen," a documentary on the Colorado summer festival, which included performances by pianist Misha Dicter and violinists Itzhak Perlmann and Pinchas Zuckerman. A second major category absent at 9 p.m. was film. But before the evening was over, a movie buff could have seen Don Ameche invent the telephone in the 1939 "Story of Alexander Graham Bell"; an Alfred Hitchcock thriller, "Marnie"; the 1945 John Wayne western "Dakota"; Irene Dunne in "I Remember Mama"; Gary Cooper as "Good Sam"; as well as an Abbott and Costello comedy, a Vincent Price horror film, and a 1933 Tarzan movie with Buster Crabbe.

During that same day, Bay Area television stations had offered sports fans the two National Football League conference championships and (on public television) tennis matches from the Spalding World Mixed-Doubles Championship. There were also ethnically-oriented programs for the Chicano, Black, Italian, and German communities. Finally, there were discussions and documentaries on the energy crisis, population problems in Latin America, vegetarianism, alcoholism, and several Bicentennial-related subjects—as well as an assortment of religious programs, half-a-dozen wildlife films, an analysis of the International Women's Year Conference, and a report on attempts by geologists to predict earthquakes.

By any measure, these programs represent a remarkably rich cross-section of American culture. This may be a particularly varied sample of programs, but it is not atypical. (Most unusual is the presence of the "ABC Theater," a "special" which substituted for the regularly scheduled "ABC Sunday Night Movie." But in this bicentennial year, history—and especially historical drama—is becoming almost a staple on commercial as well as public television.) Nor is this variety confined to a few areas of the country. Fully 60 percent of the country's homes are capable of receiving seven or more signals off the air.[5] Thus, even without cable, a majority of Americans now have access to an abundance of television.

Intimacy

It has been frequently noted that television is a peculiarly intimate medium. It is part of the domestic scene, its use interwoven into the texture of daily life. One's relationship to television is more like one's relationship to the newspaper—or to a neighbor—than to film or play, which are experienced outside of the daily routine. We turn the set on casually; we rarely attend to it with full concentration. It is generally permissible to talk or carry out other activities in its presence. The inevitable commercial interruptions virtually preclude prolonged absorption.

Yet, if we are not intense viewers, most of us are faithful viewers. At 9 p.m. on a Sunday evening in winter, for example, television sets will be on in slightly more than two-thirds of all homes in the country.[6] Television does more than inform and entertain us—its ubiquitous presence helps us regulate our lives. The progression of news-time, prime-time, bedtime (or the late show for insomniacs) is a pattern which defines the evening for vast numbers of Americans. The highly structured routines of half-hour and hour programs, as well as the equally structured weekly schedule, serves as a kind of implicit clock and calendar, even when we are not watching.

For all these reasons, we tend not to subject television to critical scrutiny—to compare one program with another, or to evaluate it against a set of explicit standards. While we are taught from an early age to be critical readers, we learn at an even earlier age that television is watched without reflection. We are seldom moved to analyze what we have seen, to raise such questions as:

What was the moral of the story I have just watched? (Even brief consideration of a television program often leads to the realization that the implicit message, as in many art forms, is quite different from the explicit one.) Did the visual images—say, in a news story—reinforce, distract from, or contradict the spoken text? If the images did carry a different message, what was it?

Thus, the television critic is faced with a dual challenge. In order to raise such pertinent questions, he must learn to abstract himself from the normally unreflective relationship between viewer and medium. But if he is to remain true to the special qualities of the medium, he must not lose touch with the nature of what Benjamin DeMott has called "the viewer's experience."

Flow

A book has a tangible physical existence. Films and plays begin and end in darkness and silence, which allow them to stand on their own. Television programs, by contrast, are surrounded by commercials and other programs. The English writer Raymond Williams has described this uninterrupted following of one thing by another as "flow," a characteristic which he believes to be central to the television experience, yet about which "it is very difficult to say anything." The reason for this difficulty, he explains, is that "it is a characteristic for which hardly any of our received modes of observation and description prepare us."[7]

One result of this flow is a powerful tendency to blur the contents of television together. To some degree, this tendency is encouraged by the network and station planners, who design their schedules specifically so that one program leads effortlessly into the next. We frequently will tune into television at an arbitrary time, watch for awhile, then tune out again at an equally arbitrary time. The goal of the programmer, of course, is to persuade us to stay tuned in for as long as possible.

The critic's problem is to decide what to isolate from this flow. Usually, he considers a single program (typically the first episode of a new series) as if it were a movie or a play, treating it as an autonomous whole. While appropriate for other media, this approach is wrong for television on two counts: First, each program interacts with those around it, and, second, most programs are really parts of continuing series rather than isolated works. In virtually every category of program—comedy, adventure drama, soap opera, quiz show—the continuing series is a recurring pattern. It is, in fact, one of the basic forms of the medium.

This suggests that the television audience derives as much pleasure from familiarity as from novelty. The viewer's enjoyment of new episodes in a series is enhanced by his memory of previous episodes. This sense of familiarity is further reinforced by the intimate nature of the viewer's relationship with the medium and by the unique impact of the lead characters in television series. These series characters are knowable as in no other medium. In order to survive exposure and maintain the audience's interest and sympathy in scores of episodes, a character must strike a deeply responsive chord in millions of viewers.

The number of characters who are able to do this is relatively small. Matt Dillon and Joe Friday, Ernie Bilko and Ralph Kramden, Marcus Welby and Perry Mason, Kojak and Columbo, Archie Bunker and Mary Tyler Moore are a few who have managed to attain places of considerable importance for themselves in the American popular imagination. They are all creations as substantial and memorable as the plots in which they performed were evanescent and forgettable. They have taken on an existence and meaning which cannot be accounted for by any single episode, because the audience's acquaintance with them is acquired gradually over a period of years.

The performers who embody these characters are, I believe, the key creative figures in the medium, and the nature of their art is worth serious examination by the critics. One of its most striking aspects is the completeness with which these characters are identified with actors or actresses who portray them. It is impossible, for example, to imagine Bilko apart from Phil Silvers or Kojak apart from Telly Savalas. And it is no coincidence that "All In The Family," still the most popular series on television after five years, is referred to almost interchangeably as "Archie Bunker."

This is one more dimension which differentiates television from theater and film. In theater, the successful realization of a play is primarily a collaboration between playwright and director, while film (especially since the demise of the star system) is widely recognized as a director's medium. But in television, both writer and director must serve the performer. A long-running series will typically utilize the services of a number of directors and, perhaps, scores of writers; but it is the relatively few central series characters who provide the central thread of continuity. The energy and style which performers like Carroll O'Connor, Telly Savalas or Mary Tyler Moore bring to their roles are the core upon which all other elements of a series depend.

The importance of the performer's role extends even to television news. In addition to their reportorial skills, the best known television journalists—one thinks especially of Cronkite and Chancellor—can also be seen as successfully created personae. Because the content (that is, the news stories covered and the information conveyed) is so similar among the network news programs, style is often the element which determines viewer loyalties. Personally, I find that on days of momentous events I prefer Cronkite's oracular delivery while on days marked only by the small occurences which fill the interstices of history, Chancellor's laconic style seems more congenial.

When attacked for the power of their positions, television journalists are fond of describing themselves as messengers (who, they add, should not be blamed if the messages they bear happen to contain bad news). But when these messengers become as famous in their own right as the public figures their messages concern, then the appropriateness of this description becomes dubious indeed. The point is not that the dramatic appeal of television journalists compromises their reliability, any more than the development of a distinctive "voice" by a print journalist destroys his credibility. But to ignore this dramatic element is to distort the actual nature of the television experience.

Criticism which fails to take these special characteristics of television into account is unlikely to make contact with the realities of the viewer's experience. What is needed is a critic who is willing to suspend judgment until he has developed a working knowledge of a program—its characters, typical plots, and controlling conventions. He would then be able to describe the structure of dramatic premises which give the program continuity and to assess the dimensions of the world it presents. Only after repeated viewings will the critic be able to answer such questions as: Are the characters appealing and interesting enough to sustain viewer loyalty? Does the program maintain a high level of craftsmanship in writing, directing and acting? Are its basic premises sufficiently broad so that the pleasures it provides are not merely redundant, but cumulative? Or (in the case of news) how do the personalities of the reporters and the dramatic structure of their presentations affect the information they convey?

Of course, there is also need for immediate reviews of new

programs. This sort of criticism, typically found in the daily newspaper columns, provides useful guidance as to what to seek out and what to miss in the flood of available programs. This function will become even more important as the number of channels and choices increases. But such immediate reviews cannot substitute for a more deliberate criticism which raises fundamental questions about the medium or deals with basic program elements which are only revealed over time.

Simplicity

In his *Studies in Classic American Literature*, D. H. Lawrence warns of the "duplicity" of American art: "You must look through the surface," he tells us, "otherwise it's all mere childishness." The explicit message is always clear, positive, and pious, but a deeper, more compelling meaning lurks beneath it. Lawrence's thesis applies to American television programming as well. On the surface, much of the medium's content appears so simple that it is transparent, so simple there seems to be little that can be said about it. On more careful examination, however, complexities begin to appear —complexities of character, of theme, and of symbolic meaning.

Many characteristics of this medium favor simplicity of form: Its domestic setting discourages undivided attention, which complexity of story requires. The television screen's small size and low resolution precludes visual complexity and the need to compress complete stories into hours and half-hours requires the elimination of all but the most essential elements. The medium's unrelenting appetite for material forces a reliance on formula and convention. However, the most powerful force favoring simplicity is, once again, the mass nature of the medium. In order to attract and hold an audience of millions, a successful national program must find subjects and characters whose appeal cuts across enormous variations in education, class, age, locale, and interests.

It is the mass nature of television—and its attendant requirements—which brings us to the heart of the problem of television criticism. The standard, pejorative description of the television's universailty is that it is aimed at the audience's "lowest common denominator"—implying that "lowest" refers to aesthetic quality. Television, it is said, is merely a vehicle for purely "escapist" fare, slickly crafted but devoid of any qualities which deserve serious attention.

Certainly, much of what appears on television is mediocre or worse. But the same is true of every medium, every art form. Ironically, it may be that television has been judged and found wanting by a set of standards higher than those applied to other media. Neil Postman of New York University has argued that when a medium "saturate[s] the culture in a cumulative way like television, people have their expectations exaggerated to such an extent they tend to apply unrealistic criteria." Because television is always available at the turn of a switch, we tend to sample more of it and expect that it will satisfy us when we want it. As a result, Postman suggests, "people think television should have a substantially higher percentage of what they construe as quality shows than any other medium. It is a demand which no medium could meet."[8]

The Shaping Forces of Television

What succeeds or fails on television is to some degree determined by the technical characteristics of the medium. Thus, the small screen severely limits the effectiveness of spectacle, but is appropriate for more intimate kinds of drama. Similarly, television's low-fidelity sound has discouraged the use of the medium for music, while its instantaneous transmission has made television an ideal vehicle for sports, news, and certain public affairs events.

There are, however, two other determinants of the purposes for which television will or will not be used.[9] The first is the nature of the institutions that control the medium. Because of the particular way the medium evolved in this country, American television is dominated by three national commercial networks. Together, they account for nearly 90 percent of all viewing time. (Their actual influence is even greater than this figure suggests, since much of the programming on independent stations consists of reruns of programs originally produced for network distribution.) Commercial networks and stations are, of course, profit-making institutions. Their income is derived from advertising revenues, which depend on the number of viewers. Their goal—to oversimplify, but only slightly—is to attract the largest possible audience, which dictates a policy of mass entertainment programming. Thus, the television programming available in this country is largely determined by the competition among these organizations for a dominant share of the audience.

Because programming (and, hence, commercial) time is limited, and because the stakes are high—gross network advertising revenues for 1974 were slightly more than $2 billion—the three networks have been notoriously unhospitable to experiment or innovation. Especially in prime-time, the networks have concentrated on elaborations and variations of a relatively limited number of well-proven dramatic formulae—domestic comedies, westerns, crime dramas, medical shows, etc. It is difficult to believe that the television audience would not only accept but welcome a wider range of subjects and forms.

The place where experimentation is most often found is public television. Since noncommercial stations are funded to provide a public service, they are able to offer programming for more specialized interests. Unfortunately, American public television has suffered from the chronic handicaps of under-financing and an inability to define a coherent programming policy. While Nielsen ratings may be an inadequate measure of a public television program's success, the public broadcasting system has failed to develop alternative standards for judging the effectiveness of its programs. Until it solves these persistent problems, public television is unlikely to become a major force capable of competing vigorously, as it should, with commercial television.

The final determinant of the content of any television system is the nature of the society of which it is a part. Thus, the high quality of historical television drama from Britain cannot be accounted for simply by the cultural superiority of the BBC (actually, much of the historical drama from England seen in this country is produced by their commercial networks, not the BBC). Rather, the events of the past, and their interpretation, continue to be subjects of popular interest, and British television both reflects and responds to that interest.

Much the same is true of the prevalence of violence in American television. The ubiquity of that motif in American film, literature, and even in the news, suggests that violence must be understood as a characteristic of the society, not merely of television. This is not to say that the *effect* of televised violence is not a legitimate subject for concern. But to treat television as if it were isolated from the surrounding society is a fundamental error. The many ways that television interacts with society—both as a reflector of its values and interests and as an active shaping influence upon them—is a recurring theme of the essays in this volume.

Television as Mediator

The objective of the Aspen Television Workshop has been to examine the best that television has to offer—not the achievements of isolated "specials" but the successes of the most interesting continuing series. We focused primarily on prime-time programs since that is where the greatest effort is expended by broadcasters and where most of the audience is. Although the prime-time hours (7:30-11:00 p.m., Monday through Sunday) make up only 15 percent of the broadcast week, they account for nearly 40 percent of total viewing time.[10]

The essays in this volume demonstrate, I believe, that television fare does deserve serious attention. The authors recognize that television's diverse audience is not interested in instruction or inspiration but in entertainment. However, in order to hold the loyalty of this audience, programs must relate to their interests and concerns. The essays suggest that every successful program, including the comedies, "connects" with its audiences by embodying their concerns in dramatic form.

If there is a single theme which unifies this volume, it is that television is not simply a "medium" but a "mediator"—between fact and fantasy; between our desire to escape and our need to deal with real problems; between our old values and new ideas; between our individual lives and the life of the nation and the world. Seen from this perspective, television becomes much more interesting and much less simple than before.

This dual nature of television is dealt with most explicitly in the essay by Peter Wood, who argues that television functions for the society as dreams do for the individual. Through displaced events and disguised characters, society uses television drama as a means of transforming its fears and unresolved problems into metaphorical forms which are less threatening than direct confrontation. (By analogy, his essay suggests another reason we have failed to develop a serious television criticism: the medium may be so important to us, on a deep level, that we instinctively resist subjecting our television experience to conscious analysis.)

Although their approaches are more traditional, Kenneth Pierce and Paula Fass argue that television comedy provides more than escapist humor. Pierce sees "All In The Family"* as a representation of the struggle to cope with the relentless pressure of social change. He speculates that the universality of this dilemma accounts for the broad and lasting popularity of the program. From her perspective as a cultural historian, Fass characterizes "The Mary Tyler Moore Show" and "M*A*S*H" as contemporary versions of a basic historical conflict: the impulse toward individualism versus the need for cooperation in a complex society. This theme, also found in the works of Cooper, Melville, and Twain, places these two shows in the mainstream of American mythology.

David Thorburn's essay on television melodrama picks up the theme of the importance of performance in the medium. Noting an apparent contradiction between the implausibility of television plots and the realism of acting within them, Thorburn presents the paradoxical proposition that "television melodrama often becomes more truthful as it becomes more implausible." He compares the structures of series such as "Medical Center" and "Kojak" to the works of Dickens and grand opera, in which complexity of plot exists as a setting for the expression of heightened but real emotions.

The subject of Robert Alley's essay is the history of television's medical shows, from "Medic" in the early 1950s through the current examples, "Marcus Welby, M.D." and "Medical Center." Throughout the genre, Alley finds a tension between our almost superstitious desire to see doctors as infallible heroes, protecting us from illness and death, and the recognition that physicians are as imperfect and mortal as the rest of us. Alley sees the balance tipping slowly in favor of greater realism, but he attributes the recent cancellation of the highly iconoclastic "Medical Story" to the audience's continued reluctance to abandon their faith in medical practitioners.

Like Alley, Kevin Ryan is interested in the relationship between television drama and viewers' values. His essay is an experimental attempt to use Lawrence Kohlberg's theory of moral development to analyze the content of an episode of "Kung Fu" (the same episode which Peter Wood subjects to psychoanalytic interpretation in his essay). Ryan believes that Kohlberg's work provides a useful means for assessing the messages and morality of television drama, as well as determining whether their impact on the audience is

---

*The discussion of this series, and other series elsewhere in the book, are based primarily on programs broadcast during the 1974-75 season.

pro-social or anti-social.

Sharon Sperry examines the narrative and dramatic qualities of a different genre, television news. She demonstrates that the television news "story" utilizes many of the same dramatic conventions as the fictional stories presented by that medium. While the use of such devices may seem illegitimate as journalism, she suggests the tendency is inevitable. At its best, the TV news story strikes an effective balance between the faithful representation of complex realities and the need to simplify and dramatize. However, Sperry does believe some changes are called for if television news is to be as effective at informing as it is at entertaining the viewers.

Finally, David Littlejohn contributes an essay on the state of television criticism. Based on an extensive survey of writings published in magazines and newspapers over the past 25 years, Littlejohn discusses the problems, the accomplishments, and the shortcomings of the television criticism practiced in this country. After reviewing the history of American television criticism, Littlejohn speculates about its future: he proposes a series of topics and approaches which he believes deserve to be given greater attention, and concludes by sketching a profile of what he considers the qualities of the ideal television critic.

John Leonard (who writes about television under the name "Cyclops") claims that "television is now our only way of talking to each other about who we think we are."[11] What he means, I think, is that television has become not only our primary channel for information about the world, but also the principal source of the imaginative forms through which we interpret this information and our own experiences. If he is right, then we can no longer afford to ignore what the medium is saying to us. Certainly, television has its flaws, but so does the society we live in. And until we begin to take television seriously, there is no hope of making it better. Our first steps must be to watch it carefully, to think about what we're seeing, to find a language to describe what we see accurately and, only then, to pass judgment.

Of our misunderstanding of American literature, D. H. Lawrence explained that "it is hard to hear a new voice, as hard as it is to listen to an unknown language. We just don't listen." Wouldn't it be remarkable if, right before our eyes, American television was trying to tell us as much about ourselves as we can bear to know?

Footnotes

1. George Comstock and Marilyn Fisher, *Television and Human Behavior: A Guide to the Pertinent Scientific Literature.* Santa Monica: The Rand Corporation, Report R-1746-CF, June 1975.

2. Horace Newcomb, *TV: The Most Popular Art.* Garden City: Anchor Press/Doubleday, 1974 (paperback), page 1.

3. The description of television as a "vast wasteland" was originally used in the eariy 1960s by Newton Minow, then chairman of the Federal Communications Commission.

4. Program listings taken from *TV Guide*, January 3-9, 1976. Channels 36 and 54 are located in San Jose. But all stations listed (as well as channel 11, also in San Jose, which duplicated the programming on channel 7) were easily obtainable off the air—with an indoor set-top antenna in Palo Alto, approximately 40 miles south of San Francisco.

5. *Nielsen Television '73*, Chicago: A. C. Nielsen Company.

6. *Nielsen Television '75*, Chicago: A. C. Nielsen Company, page 7.

7. Raymond Williams, *Television: Technology and Cultural Form.* New York: Schocken Books, 1975, page 95.

8. Quoted by Marvin Kitman, "Recalling Past Misfires," *Newsday*, Sunday, January 18, 1976.

9. This account of the factors shaping television content is based on the work of Raymond Williams. See *Television: Technology and Cultural Form.*

10. *Nielsen Television '75*, page 10.

11. William Severini Kowinski, "Cyclops: man with one eye in the land of the blind," *TeleVISIONS*, October/November 1975, page 4.

Television as Dream

Peter H. Wood

There are dreams as distinct as actual experiences, so distinct that for some time after waking we do not realize that they were dreams at all; others, which are ineffably faint, shadowy and blurred; in one and the same dream, even, there may be some parts of extraordinary vividness alternating with others so indistinct as to be almost wholly elusive. Again, dreams may be quite consistent or at any rate coherent, or even witty or fantastically beautiful; others again are confused, apparently imbecile, absurd or often absolutely mad. There are dreams which leave us quite cold, others in which every affect makes itself felt—pain to the point of tears, terror so intense as to wake us, amazement, delight, and so on. Most dreams are forgotten soon after waking; or

Mr. Wood, author of *Black Majority* (Knopf, 1974), lives in Hillsborough, N.C., and teaches early American history at Duke. As Assistant Director of Humanities for the Rockefeller Foundation in the early '70s he developed a strong interest in video and served as writer/editor for a Public Television special, "Human Rights—Human Reality." A condensed version of "Television as Dream" appeared in *American Film* (December, 1975).

they persist throughout the day, the recollection becoming fainter and more imperfect as the day goes on;
others remain so vivid (as, for example, the dreams of
childhood) that thirty years later we remember them as
clearly as though they were part of a recent experience.
Dreams, like people, may make their appearances once
and never come back; or the same person may dream the
same thing repeatedly, either in the same form or with
slight alterations. In short, these scraps of mental activity
at night-time have at command an immense repertory,
can in fact create everything that by day the mind is
capable of—only, it is never the same.[1]

—Sigmund Freud

Not long ago the austere American diplomat and scholar,
George F. Kennan, commiserated with a group of Oxford and
Cambridge graduates that they lived in a world changing too fast for
its own good. It is "a world," Kennan moralized, "given increasingly
to the primitive delights of visual communication."

Ever since monks stopped illuminating their manuscripts and
turned to the dull efficiencies of the printing press, academics and
other bibliophiles have taken a condescending stance toward any
non-linear forms of information exchange. Particularly offensive to
shareholders in the print economy is television, that newest process
of illumination which changes light into an electrical image and back
to light again. There is something threatening, confusing, paralyzing
about its "primitive delights"; it is a bad dream, and they wish it
would go away.

But George Kennan and all the king's men could never devise an
adequate "containment theory" for American television. The cornu-
copia-shaped tube is in 98 percent of American dwellings, and, for
at least a quarter of every day, it is scanning electrons toward us at a
rate of over 30,000 lines per second. It has become a real and permanent fixture in our homes and in our heads. TV is no dream. Or
is it?

If television is not the meaningless nightmare deplored by
numerous elders, could it in fact be something of the inverse: a
significant flow of collective dream materials which we have not yet
begun to interpret adequately? Most of us can recall incidents where
television contributed to our own dreams. (After all, TV frequently

serves to put us to sleep these days—both figuratively and literally.) And the recent Surgeon General's report on TV violence even hinted at simple substitution, reporting that those who watch more TV dream less. But if we can accept the idea that TV *affects* the dream-life of individuals, can we entertain the thought that TV may also *constitute*—in some unrecognized way—part of the collective dream-life of society as a whole? Is there room, in other words, for *the interpretation of television as dream*?

A few people are beginning to think so. A recent issue of the California bulletin, *Dreams and Inner Spaces*, for example, dealt with the parallels between dreams and TV. Among those who have already considered this concept, the most notable is anthropologist Ted Carpenter. Carpenter has co-edited *Explorations in Communication* with Marshall McLuhan, and written a book called *They Became What They Beheld* (not about television!) with photographer Ken Hyman. The fall 1972 issue of *Television Quarterly* carried a piece by communications professor John Carden entitled, "Reality and Television: An Interview with Dr. Edmund Carpenter," in which Carpenter suggests that the viewer of media events "participates solely as dreamer." He observes that, "Television is the real psychic leap of our time. ...Its content is the stuff of dreams and its form is pure dream."

If there are grounds for such an approach, as I myself am increasingly convinced, then it bears directly on the concept which we accept as "TV criticism" (or, more significantly, "TV analysis"). Therefore, one point should be stressed at the outset: raising the prospect of analyzing "TV as dream" does not in any way negate traditional approaches to television. If valid, it would necessarily reinforce existing modes of media criticism. It would neither supplant them nor be irrelevant to them; it would simply offer an additional related perspective.

Where does TV criticism stand now? To some it seems suitably rich and diversified; to others it appears depressingly homogenized and inconsequential. But value judgments aside, almost *all* current criticism falls into one or both of the following modes: art commentary, or industry commentary. Stated another way, TV criticism, as it presently exists, derives from two sources: traditional artistic and literary criticism on the one hand, and the modern newspaper-magazine genre which might be called "Hollywood commentary" on the other.

The artistic or cultural approach, though by no means highbrow, involves a slight distancing from the material. It addresses matters drawn from traditional art forms, particularly drama, such as the subtlety of the story line and the skill of the actors. Unfortunately, as Marvin Barrett of the Columbia School of Journalism points out, most network shows measured on these scales "don't even register in the aesthetic area." The TV critic applying traditional dramatic and cultural standards confronts, in Barrett's phrase, "continuous mediocrity." But if the Marvin Barretts dread and deprecate such mediocrity, the Rona Barretts extol and expand it. The mode of industry criticism which has grown up around film, TV's celluloid godparent, shapes a vast range of television commentary. It encompasses both pure network handouts and hard-nosed exposés. But whether adulatory or critical, intimate or detached, this mode depends upon at least an appearance of investigative reporting and it overflows with personal and production details. "Which people?" "What expenses?" "Why—when—how?" It is the "low-down" by and for the would-be insider.

As much as anything else, it is these two roots, epitomized by drama criticism and Hollywood coverage, which have given TV analysis its current shape. From the former, it derives a strongly judgmental and crudely critical tone. Appraisers of prime-time television make heavy use of such words as "good" and "bad," "should" and "shouldn't," far beyond their limited role as consumer counsellors. From the latter, TV analysis derives a directness, a narrowness, a literal-mindedness. There is a willingness to deal with separate segments of shows or personalities in isolation; there is a tendency to accept, and even stress, surface appearances. While other ways to categorize TV criticism are obviously available, anyone doubting the existence of these two roots can examine them, thoroughly entwined, in a publication such as TV Guide.

Commenting along these lines in the interview mentioned above, Ted Carpenter stated:

> I'm convinced that we judge television as if it were a modified form of print—and, of course, find it wanting. What we overlook is the reality it reveals. Unlike print, television doesn't transmit bits of information. Instead it *transports* the viewer. . . .*All television becomes dream.* This is the inner trip, the search for meaning beyond the world of daily appearance.

The question being posed below is whether art analysis and industry analysis of TV could not be complemented by a new and separate form of "dream analysis," a form which might take us, in Carpenter's words, "beyond the world of daily appearance."

Before addressing this serious question directly, consider it in a playfully inverted form: what could current television analysts tell you about the workings of your individual subconscious? Suppose for a moment the TV critics' tendencies to stress surface content and to emphasize value judgments were applied to the interpretation of your own dreams. The results, of course, would be ludicrous. To learn that a given dream was a "tedious rerun," containing "entirely too much sex, though humorous in places," would provide limited enlightenment at best. For in dream interpretation, the "originality" of the plot and dialogue, the "level" of acting, the "uniqueness" of the characters, the "realism" of the setting, and the "logic" of the ending all become matters of little or no relevance. In short, the questions which are currently deemed most appropriate, useful, and legitimate in TV analysis are the very ones which seem most inappropriate, useless, and illegitimate in dream analysis.

But if dream interpretation can have anything to offer television, basic similarities between TV and dream must first be established. Therefore, begin by considering a list of half a dozen general congruities:

1. *Both TV and dreams have a highly visual quality.* The word "tele-vision" and the much older medieval phrase "dream vision" underscore this point. "In dreams we go through many experiences," Freud wrote in his *General Introduction to Psychoanalysis.* "For the most part our experiences take the form of visual images; there may be feeling as well, thoughts, too, mixed up with them, and the other senses may be drawn in; but for the most part dreams consist of visual images."

2. *Both TV and dreams are highly symbolic.* As Michael Arlen noted in an excellent *New Yorker* column (April 7, 1975), TV "transforms experience into symbols" in accordance with an incessant and deeply felt human need. Dreams do the same. "Symbolism," Freud stated, "is perhaps the most remarkable part of our theory of dreams."

3. *Both TV and dreams involve a high degree of wish-fulfillment.* The enemies and the exponents of television, for different reasons, have acknowledged the degree to which the medium provides an escape and a release into a world of fantasy—fantasy which often

gains its power as a heightened and intensified version of reality. "That dreams are brought about by a wish and that the content of the dream expresses this wish," Freud wrote, "is one main characteristic of dreams." He continued, "the dream does not merely give expression to a thought, but represents this wish as fulfilled, in the form of an hallucinatory experience." It is "almost like being there" in each instance, living through some form of an experience which is greatly desired or—equally important and not entirely opposite— which is greatly feared. Thus real and implied violence has a heightened place in both the prime-time dreaming of individuals and the prime-time television of our culture. Chase scenes and sexual hints are as commonplace in one as in the other.

4. *Both TV and dreams appear to contain much that is disjointed and trivial.* But the contents of dreams, and perhaps someday of television, can be shown to be consistent and coherent. We have all heard TV content dismissed vehemently as being beneath serious concern, much as Freud once heard verbal slips and then dreams dismissed. "A certain element of exaggeration in a criticism may arouse our suspicions," he wrote, intrigued as always by the implications of resistance. "The arguments brought against the dream as an object of scientific research are clearly extreme. We have met with the objection of triviality already in 'errors,' and have told ourselves that great things may be revealed by small indications." It will take time and patience to determine which—if any—great things stand to be revealed by the trivia of prime-time television.

5. *Both TV and dreams have an enormous and powerful content, most of which is readily and thoroughly forgotten.* Freud wrote that, "Most dreams cannot be remembered at all and are forgotten except for some tiny fragments." It is relatively easy, and apparently necessary, for individual dreamers to avoid or forget much of the content of most of their dreams. They are able, at least with effort and practice, to awaken from dreams they cannot handle. However, they are also able to return to and recall dreams with which they are ready to deal. Avoiding conscious recollection of a dream does not erase its content; the themes continue to recur and impinge. All this is quite similar with television, where avoidance mechanisms (beyond direct forgetfulness) function at a variety of levels from living room channel switching to FCC censorship. (It may not be surprising that Timothy Leary and others who began experimenting with non-sleep dreaming through drugs adopted a terminology drawn from television: "turn on," "tune in," "turn off.") Is it conceivable

that television, like dreams, could be repetitive, boring, and mundane on the surface precisely because its latent content is so relevant, powerful, and pervasive?

6. *Finally, both TV and dreams make consistent use—overt and disguised—of materials drawn from recent experience.* Freud stated in the *General Introduction* that, "we want to know further from what cause and to what end we repeat in dreams this which is known to us and has recently happened to us." We wish to know much the same thing about television. Like dream, television's brief and non-linear visual images invoke—and also evoke—a great wealth of familiar and often current material stored in the viewer's mind.

If, for the sake of experimentation or argument, one goes along with all or most of these rough generalizations, an interesting and somewhat heretical critical perspective begins to open up. But to explore it depends upon the tentative acceptance, or at least upon the consideration, of two further and somewhat novel assumptions. The first has to do with whether television is—as we often more than half seriously say it is—a "mindless" phenomenon.

When Freud began his consideration of dreams in the 1890s, others had been involved in related speculations for several decades. But their conclusions (not unlike those of the first generation of TV critics) tended to stress the ways in which dream failed to measure up to reality. Freud wrote that, "they are content with the bare enumeration of the divergences of the dream-life from waking thought with a view to depreciating the dreams: they emphasize the lack of connection in the associations, the suspended exercise of the critical faculty, the elimination of all knowledge, and other indications of diminished functioning." The mind, they concluded, was at rest, too relaxed to "make sense"; dreams were therefore to be understood in somatic or bodily terms. It was Freud's insight to turn this assumption upside down: "let us accept as the basis of the whole of our further enquiry the following hypothesis—that dreams are not a somatic, but a mental phenomenon." He went on to ask, "but what is our justification in making this assumption? We have none, but on the other hand there is nothing to prevent us."

Where lack of sense, lack of importance or meaning, had been assumed, Freud postulated the opposite. What happens if we make the same assumption about TV, using the same justification at first —that is, "there is nothing to prevent us"? In so doing, we set aside, for the moment, somatic interpretations of television (TV as SOMA?)

which stress the physical origins and characteristics of each show, series, or network, much less of the medium as a whole. We assume that beyond inadvertency ("Some guy just came up with that line," or "The tight budget meant they just happened to cut the scene here"), and beyond specificity ("Peter Falk always acts that way," or "All Norman Lear shows are like that"), there also exists some larger consciousness to which television can be linked.

But what is this collective consciousness which at some level can be said to create and consume the images of television? Here we must add a second hypothesis. Just as our dreams, contrary to traditional logic, have been proven to be the product of our individual subconscious, so perhaps TV may eventually be understood as a form of dream-equivalent within the "collective subconscious." I do not employ this last phrase in any strict parallel to Jung's similar term, although it is suggestive that TV is built around archetypes, many of them similar to the primordial images which Jung believed to be stored in the "collective unconscious" of the entire species. Instead I refer, for the moment, to the entity of our own American society, virtually all of whose homes are reached by television. It is the hypothesis that, within this entity, whatever can be said validly on one level about the separate consciousness of distinctive and discernible audiences, producers, etc., something else can be said on another level about the consciousness of the entire entity as a whole. At that level such little-understood social phenomena as feedback and simultaneity and information-storage do away with the separateness of image-viewer and image-maker in a single collective consciousness, sharing simultaneously in powerful ephemeral images. To quote Ted Carpenter again:

> We live inside our media. *We* are their content. Television images come at us so fast, in such profusion, that they engulf us, tattoo us. We're immersed. It's like skin diving. We're surrounded, and whatever surrounds, involves. Television doesn't just wash over us and then "go out of mind." It goes *into* mind, deep into mind. The subconscious is a world in which we store everything, not something, and television extends the subconscious.

It is paradoxical, but also logical, that by definition this media consciousness (in which we are all infinitely small participating parts) is not aware of the workings of its collective subconscious on the surface, but only at some lower level. That is to say, if we know about it, we don't know we know, and I would argue that, to a remarkable degree, this applies just as much to the so-called "creators" as to the so-called "viewers." As Freud wrote about the creators of individual dreams, "I assure you that it is not only quite possible, but highly probable, that the dreamer really does know the meaning of his dream; *only he does not know that he knows, and therefore thinks that he does not*" (italics in original).

By implication then, and in contrast to most of what we have heard, learned, or experienced, it may be that *we ourselves are in some way responsible for television; we create it. More than any previous medium including drama and film, TV is a vivid projection of our collective subconscious.* Obviously, in practical, individual terms, we are not "responsible" for TV in whole or in part. We lack the technical understanding, the financial capacities, and perhaps even the will and insight to "create" television programs. And yet, all logic and commentary notwithstanding, we can be discovered to shape television more than it shapes us. This is true not merely in the material sense that audiences build ratings which sell products which buy programs, but also in a larger and less conscious way. Much as individuals purposefully and unconsciously create their own dream world and then react to it, I speculate that a TV society purposefully and unconsciously creates its own video world and then reacts to it.

Susan Sontag, who has speculated about the relations of dream and film, suggests in *Against Interpretation* that in one sense Freud was *too* successful in his efforts to get below the surface of things, since the influence of psychoanalysis on artistic criticism has grown overly great. But she offers a clear summary of this powerful mode: "All observable phenomena are bracketed, in Freud's phrase, as *manifest content*. This manifest content must be probed and pushed aside to find the true meaning—the *latent content*—beneath." This approach can be adapted to studying television, especially in the context of what Freud called "dream-work."

Since dreams involve repressed thoughts or wishes that cannot be handled fully or directly by the conscious individual, these hidden or latent thoughts are translated through dreaming into a series of sensory and visual images. Freud defined this transformation of a wish into a dream as "dream-work," and he referred to the opposite process of unravelling the dream-work as "interpretation." "Let me remind you," he stated with emphasis, "that *the process by which the latent dream is transformed into the manifest dream is called THE DREAM-WORK*; while the reverse process, which seeks to progress from the manifest to the latent thoughts, is our work of interpretation; the work of interpretation therefore aims at demolishing the dream-work." It was as though a powerful message was translated into an acceptable code for presentation, so that the presentation itself could then be decoded in order to discover the original message.

According to Freud, the original coding process, the dream-work, proceeds through several different means. The first and most self-explanatory means is *condensation*, the process of compressing, combining, fragmenting, or omitting elements of the latent thoughts as they become content in the manifest dream. The second means is *displacement*, whereby "a latent element may be *replaced*, not by a part of itself, but by something more remote, something of the nature of an allusion," or "the *accent* may be transferred from an important element to another which is unimportant, so that the center of the dream is shifted as it were, giving the dream a foreign appearance." A third means, sometimes labelled *inversion*, involves both the "regressive translation of thoughts into images" and also the fact that these visual images themselves are often "inverted," containing multiple, contradictory or opposite meanings. An ambiguity, an ambivalence, is set up, the consideration of which can be an important aspect of interpretation. A fourth element of dream-work, implicit in each of the preceding three, might be called *dramatization*, for the transformation of latent thoughts into manifest dreams involves continuous and inclusive working of material into some dramatic form, whether vivid or sketchy, polished or loose, elaborate or mundane.

What is striking about these central aspects of dream-work is that they all apply with uncanny directness to television. If we can accept the earlier hypotheses (and, admittedly, they are difficult to concede at first, whether taken literally or metaphorically) that media society as a whole has a consciousness somewhat like that of an individual, and that one way this collective consciousness deals with latent thoughts is by transforming them into the manifest content of television, then each separate process of dream-work can be seen to have its equivalent in what we might choose to call "TV-work."

Each of these correlations can be illustrated briefly. It goes without saying, first of all, that *TV-work involves dramatization.*

What applies to "Kojak" or "The Waltons," to Norman Lear and Associates or Mary Tyler Moore Productions, also applies to the creations of "CBS News" and "ABC Sports"; all prime-time television partakes heavily of drama. But it is less the drama of a playwright, with continuity which allows development, than the drama of a dream, with immediacy which provides belief. "Television," Carpenter states, "seems complete in itself. Each television experience seems distinct, self-sufficient, utterly true as itself, judged and motivated and understood in terms of itself alone. Concepts such as causation and purpose appear irrelevant."

Secondly, *TV-work involves condensation*—drastic, continuous and creative condensation. To take simply one example, Rhoda Morganstern of "Rhoda" is introduced as a "window decorator." This single tag, while entirely plausible and mundane in itself, is rich in associative meanings along several dimensions (just as Art Carney on "The Honeymooners" used to work in the sewers). Rhoda is pretty enough to be a window decoration herself, but she is also competent enough to decorate windows. That is, she has a useful money-earning job outside the home, yet the job is strikingly similar in content to traditional unpaid work within the home. In fact, "window decorating" connotes on one level all that is regarded as superficial, transparent and peripheral about women's traditional roles. However, on another level, it connotes central aspects of female sexuality presented as decorous virginity. And so on.

Also, *TV-work involves displacement* (and it is interesting to assume in this regard, as one does with dreams, that the more jumbled or obscure a presentation seems to be, the more displacement there has been in the process of TV-work). As a simple example, consider an element of a recent "Mary Tyler Moore Show" episode in which Mary finds herself serving dinner to Lou, her manly but insecure middle-aged "boss." (In condensed TV, as in condensed dream, one often "finds oneself" doing something with limited lead-in or prior explanation.) Much of "MTM" deals with displaced sexual wishes—the show is introduced by a song about "making it"—though this scene is more apparent than most. Among the things Mary wants to have at this Friday night rendezvous is a bottle of champagne, and the visual imagery and verbal dialogue of the scene, heavy with double meanings, focuses around how to open the bottle satisfactorily. Lou, uncertain but pretending to know how to do it, receives friendly encouragement and guidance from the more experienced and competent Mary. When he finally holds the large bottle erect in front of him and uncorks it, the prized white liquid comes bubbling out, giving Mary pleasure and transforming Lou's anxiety to satisfaction. The entire sequence, lasting only a few seconds, can be interpreted as wish fulfillment for both sexes around the prevalent concern of male impotence, all displaced in an acceptable but unmistakable way to a champagne bottle and the popping of its cork.

Lastly, *TV-work involves inversion*—the inversion of latent thoughts into meaningful and often ambiguous verbal and visual symbols, and also, to quote Freud, the "inversion of situations or of relations existing between two persons, as though the scene were laid in a 'topsy-turvy' world." "All In The Family" illustrates this point on a regular basis. Archie's steady flow of seemingly random but obviously meaningful verbal slips (such as "the infernal revenue system") are set against a series of larger situational inversions, each of which is absurd, but not *"merely"* absurd. The argumentative Bunkers function through an unending series of oppositions: male-female, young-old, white-black, liberal-conservative, us-them. . . . Yet it is significant that the presentation of contradicting arguments invariably becomes contradictory in its own right. No one ever argues a consistent "line," despite the perpetual tone of certainty. Hence, the important factor for analysis, most commentators notwithstanding, is not who comes out on which side so much as the presentation of a confusing issue. Since so much of prime-time TV deals with this kind of back-and-forth inversion, it is worth quoting Freud once again on opposites:

> One of our most surprising discoveries is the manner in which opposites in the latent dream are dealt with by the dream-work. We know already that points of agreement in the latent material are replaced by condensation in the manifest dream. Now contraries are treated in just the same way as similarities, with a marked preference for expression by means of the same manifest element. An element in the manifest dream which admits of an opposite may stand simply for itself, or for its opposite, or for both together; only the sense can decide which translation is to be chosen.

In this context, the entire question of how any given show "turns out in the end" takes on a new significance, or rather insignificance.

In the final analysis, the test of such speculations and hypotheses will be pragmatic. Their validity and usefulness must be demonstrated repeatedly over time. No one successful exercise will confirm their rightness, but then again, no single unconvincing effort will prove their wrongness. As with any propositions, we eventually accept or discard them at our own peril.

With this in mind, it seems only fair and logical to conclude with several brief attempts at specific TV analysis of the sort hinted at in the generalizations above. Let me discuss two separate shows aired during 1975, an episode of the short-lived series, "Kung Fu," and a one-hour incident from the venerable "Gunsmoke." Both are Westerns, but they are entirely different in their outward or manifest style and, I shall argue, in their primary latent content.

Take the episode of "Kung Fu" entitled *The Predators*, (described by Kevin Ryan in his essay on moral education). The story-line, or manifest content, is as follows. The Asian-American hero, Caine, stands falsely accused of killing a sheriff. Having escaped his sentence to hang, he comes across an Apache, Hoskay, whose brother has been killed by white scalp-hunters. After risking his life to protect the Indian from these bounty hunters, Caine follows them and is provoked into a conflict with the renegade Navajo, Mutala, who does much of their dirty work. In their fight Caine neutralizes his opponent and looks beyond him to the white leader, Rafe, whom he suddenly body-checks over the edge of a cliff, following after him in a dramatic free fall to the river below ("Rafe tumbling, Caine in control," according to the script). There the Apache, Hoskay, attacks Rafe in revenge. The Indian is wounded, and Caine is obliged to lead these two enemies from the canyon together. He finally succeeds, negotiating a settlement between Apaches and scalpers. In the process, he also wins an acknowledgement of his identity and wisdom from Rafe.

This story is paralleled by a sequence of flashbacks to China as young Caine watches the progress of his fellow disciple Teh Soong from youthful zealotry to the beginnings of mature self-awareness. The entire episode is built around little more than a series of unlikely fights and confrontations, the sort of dramatization from which most dreams and television are made. But more interesting is the condensation of several separate social themes from the past several years into a single plausible narrative.

The topical anxieties which provide the story's latent content are generational and racial conflict in the United States and the war in southeast Asia. Each of these themes is partially hidden by displacement. For example, the Indians in fact represent Black Americans. Hunted by rednecks (working for the man who actually killed the lawman), the Apache seeks revenge on them for killing his brother, but he hates all whites because of "all his fallen brothers." In contrast to this militant, Mutala (Mulatto?) the Navajo wears a Civil War army cap and literally fights the White Man's battle for him in the most unseemly way. He has fully accepted his role, and while it fills him with hate, this hatred is directed toward those (Caine and the Apaches) who are both more liberated and liberating.

If racial antagonisms are displaced to the West, some of those between generations are displaced to the Far East. Through the device of flashbacks to Asia, we see Teh Soong, slightly older than Caine, experience the classic student evolution of the sixties. He begins by dropping out of school. (Master Kan: "You will not be dissuaded . . . ?") His purpose is to fight injustice. (The people are living like "slaves" while the mandarins continue to "demand tribute.") While his elders seemingly do nothing, he expects to do everything. ("I will take up the cause of the people . . . I will lead them . . . speak for them . . . fight for them.") When bloodied in the movement ("beset by soldiers"), he returns to Kan's paternal care, though as young Caine observes to the Master, "Teh Soong accepts your kindness, and, at the same time, defies you." Recovered, he tries to lead the people against "the soldiers and the mandarins," only to turn from the cause and put on "the rags of a beggar," admitting openly that he had been more concerned with his own glory than with the burdens of the people.

Both of Caine's brother figures, Hoskay and Teh Soong (Ho and Tse Tung?), represent generalized aspects of anti-colonial struggle. But much of the show's dialogue concerning Vietnam is remarkably explicit. Standard words and phrases, even whole exchanges, from the war debate recur in only slightly disguised form. At the outset Rafe (Fear, but also Fa——er?) tells Caine, "Chinee, you're a caution," but proceeds to disregard him as a representative both of draftable American youth ("My father was born here") and the powerful Chinese presence. Master Kan explains of Teh Soong's radical acts, "He led a revolt in a village to the north. (sadly) Now the village has been destroyed." Note the ambiguity of the phrase "*to* the North" and also the similarity in tone and words with a well-meaning and patronizing American father (officer, editor, etc.) explaining why a village has been destroyed in order to be saved.

In the midst of these fragments from the Vietnam debate, it is worth recalling an important observation about dream dialogue. Freud claimed that *"the dream-work cannot create conversation in dreams;* save in a few exceptional cases, *it is imitated from, and made up of, things heard or even said by the dreamer himself* on the previous day, which have entered into the latent thoughts as the material or incitement of his dream" (emphasis added). Thus we hear Rafe's gun-carrying supporters say, as was often said of Uncle Sam, "I ain't seen no one lick Rafe yet." Caught in the Canyon (LBJ's tunnel?) with Caine, Rafe asks him tauntingly whether he thinks he knows the way to get out. It is a familiar American question and tone from the late sixties and early seventies and Caine's reply ("There is no choice. The way in is the way out.") paraphrases the simple and bitter response emblematic of the anti-war argument: "You can leave the way you came—in boats." But the way out is made hard when it becomes entangled in questions of "honor," whether real or pretended. "You have no honor?" Caine asks Rafe, inverting the question which older Americans had so steadily asked their young.

Equally resonant is the final dialogue between Teh Soong, returning to his studies from the resistance, and Master Kan, accepting him back, as Young Caine, who admires them both, looks on. One could hardly dream up a more succinct dramatization of the draft-resister dilemma that preoccupied Americans of the mid-seventies and that symbolized the interface between issues of generational and military conflict:

MK: Will you abide with us?
TS.   You will allow me?
MK: Our hearts are open.
TS: I beg your forgiveness, Master . . . And yours, Student Caine.
MK: You have my love.
YC: Mine as well.
TS: . . . Forgiveness?
MK: If you will find that, it must come from the one who has condemned you, Teh Soong. I would hope he would be generous. Surely there has been enough destruction.

But the latent content of a TV show is not always so heavily social; it can deal with far more personal material. This was driven home to me recently when I settled down to test out some of these ideas again at random. An episode of that most long-lived series, "Gunsmoke," had just gotten underway. A common farmer near Dodge City, legal guardian for a kindly but slow-witted younger man, is in love with a golden-haired and golden-hearted woman "working" above the Longbranch Saloon. His past is as shady as hers and as difficult to bury, when he is spotted by an old partner-in-crime who feels betrayed in a long-forgotten but unsolved bank robbery in a distant state. The farmer survives a duel with his one-time companion (the cause of which is kept from Marshal Dillon) and cements his relation to the saloon girl, only to be killed in the end by the youth for whom he holds responsibility. This devoted and dull-witted sidekick has also fallen in love with the saloon girl in his own child-like way, inspired by her beauty and her affectionate, mothering manner towards him. Needing money to "marry" her, he turns in his reformed-robber protector to Sheriff Dillon for the posted reward, not sensing the consequences for the couple he loves and depends on. Finally, overwhelmed by what he has done, the youth pulls a gun on the sheriff but shoots his unarmed benefactor instead.

In terms of "art" and "industry" criticism, I wanted an ingenious but rather far-fetched and implausible plot, conveyed better than adequately by the usual cast and aided by three talented outsiders in the feature roles. The slightly crude theme is handled creditably; overt violence, though stereotyped, is minimal; and the ending, however implausible, is suitably tragic. But what did I watch in terms of dream interpretation? The latent meaning behind the manifest content seems to be quite different and considerably more plausible. The entire hour is not only understandable, but in fact *best understood* as a direct and detailed treatment of the Oedipus Complex. It transposes to the archetypal American setting of Dodge City the universal drive summarized in the song, "I Want a Girl Just Like the Girl that Married Dear Old Dad."

Though condensation and inversion are evident, displacement is the primary element of the TV-work in this instance. In order to see the latent material clearly, it is necessary to understand that the traditional oedipal triangle has been skewed slightly—disguised—so that no one is in quite their proper role. "Father" is not the real father, only a guardian of the youth and a suitor of the saloon girl. "Mother" is not the real mother, only a kindly woman-of-the-evening who is eager to settle down. "The son" is not a real son, only a man whose slight retardedness gives him all the innocence of a child and forces him to act out, or dramatize, what others might only think.

In this context, consider three of the program's central scenes. The first scene, though ostensibly concerned with an innocent knife-game on the saloon steps, deals directly with the Son's awakening sexuality. Doc and Festus (delivering a box tied up in pink to Miss Kitty) pass the young man playing mumblety-peg, sticking his knife into the front steps of the Longbranch. He is trying to master a new feat called "over the cowshed," in which he throws his knife up in front of himself. Doc warns him not to throw it into the Longbranch and then proceeds through the (emblematic) swinging doors into the saloon-whorehouse. There he and Festus have a brief but meaningful exchange (while eyeing several prostitutes) about Doc's comparative experience and proficiency at "mumblety-peg," and the double meaning is not to Doc as a surgeon. Meanwhile, the Son tries the hard trick and pulls it off, but gets in trouble when his knife sticks close to the boots of some older men. They humiliate and taunt the young innocent by taking away his knife and passing it under and around their horses, leaving him crying in the dust until he summons his "parents" from the saloon. The scene ends when the Mother picks up the knife and restores it to the Son, while looking lovingly at the Father.

In a second central scene, the Father must undertake "man's business," which he cannot explain to his dependent, and he leaves the Son with the Mother inside the Longbranch. Her mind is elsewhere, on the man's impending (gun)fight with the old (out)law partner, but she indulges the youth's fantasies, having sworn to look after him if the male guardian is killed. When she says she would like to live in his house, he hears it innocently as an expression of sexual rather than maternal love. The forbidden oedipal wish has been stated and its fulfillment seemingly promised.

Later he is outraged when he is "treated like a kid" and denied money by his guardian and rival. His futile attempt to rob the funds he needs to be his own man and "wed" the saloon girl-Mother, brings Marshall Dillon to the house. Having innocently but ingeniously exposed his Father for robbery and won the Mother for companionship, he finally kills the person who has been the focus of his childlike anger and frustration. The forgiving Father dies lying on top of him, trying to take the smoking gun from his hand. Implausible scenes such as these, repeated endlessly each night in the privacy of our homes, may, when we get the hang of it, make more sense in psychological terms than in traditional dramatic terms.

Having suggested that the latent wishes of a generalized consciousness by means of so-called "TV-work" which bears a close resemblance to dream-work, one final question must be raised regarding any possible usefulness of this approach. Dream analysis, after all, began as, and has remained, a part of a broader process of therapy for individuals. But could the interpretation of TV as dream ever have any collective therapeutic value? The answer depends in part upon a much more thorough definition of the collective subconscious and the hows and whys of TV-work—the process of disguising societal needs and wishes in acceptable video form. The relation of each individual to this hypothetical collective consciousness will also demand further thought and speculation, as will the question, so familiar to dream analysts, of whether "working through" a fantasy periodically by some kind of mental process makes one (or in this case *all*) more aware of, and receptive toward, the underlying problem or more resigned to its continuing existence in a suppressed and unacknowledged form.

Walter Benjamin (1892-1940), the sensitive literary interpreter and cultural critic of the Frankfort School, once stated that, "During long periods of history, the mode of human sense perception changes with humanity's entire mode of existence." Benjamin, whose essays are published under the revealing title *Illuminations*, continued, "The manner in which human sense perception is organized, the medium in which it is accomplished, is determined not only by nature but by historical circumstances as well." Historical circumstances have put us in the middle of a new media world. However primitive the "delights of visual communication" may still seem to most people, it is now possible to speculate that television may someday present new and necessary "illumination" as our modes of collective perception are reorganized. After all, the video medium is young, and we have scarcely begun to understand it.

Footnotes

1. This quotation is from *A General Introduction to Psychoanalysis* (1924), p. 95 of the Pocket Book edition. Other quotations from Freud in the paper are all drawn from this same paperback edition of the *General Introduction*.

Television as Cultural Document: Promises and Problems

Paula S. Fass

Television confronts most of us regularly, as an uninvited dinner guest, the sandman of sleep, often the teacher, and, for many, a daily companion. It's a habit, a sedative, even a social mediator as it introduces us to the facts and fantasies of American society. Few media are so near and so omnipresent. Rarely does the historian have access to so much immediate experience, to such regular habits and so sustained a ritual. Perhaps its rhythms can be compared only with the tasks we associate with economic activity: the farm, the factory, the office. In this rhythmic repeated application to television viewing, we see complex facets of American culture flash by: if consumerism characterizes modern life, then television is the symbol of the consumer; if entertainment underscores our social habits, then television epitomizes entertainment; if shared social symbols are lodged in both consumerism and entertainment, then television is the powerful medium for both.

It is here, in the mass habits of the viewing public, that we find the modern communion. To be sure, television is one of the most

Ms. Fass is Assistant Professor of History at the University of California, Berkeley. Her forthcoming book, *The Damned and the Beautiful: American Youth in the 1920s* (Oxford University Press), is scheduled to appear in Spring 1977.

private of modern customs. But it is also the most public. It unites us as discrete beings into a mass audience, synchronizes our time and homogenizes our imaginations. Television is potentially the most effective resource for understanding the American popular imagination because it feeds at the same time that it reflects our social sensibilities. It provides us with choices—a kind of grand pluralism of tastes and interests—while it dictates the scope of those tastes and when they may be legitimately indulged. It is dictator and servant, barometer and filter of the popular imagination. And it is a social institution which structures our lives and unites not only our values and conventions but the minutiae of daily habits.

Because television is as much part of the rhythm of my own life as for most Americans, it is by no means easy to don the scholar's cap and to examine this social fact with the unvarnished sharp eye of scholarship, the detachment one normally brings to historical documents, to fertility curves, economic indicators, newspapers or political tracts. Not that we ever achieve an unblemished, cold and uncommitted objectivity in historical work. Usually, however, the task lends itself more easily to the removal of the scholar from the object of analysis. But, in the case of television, we not only have few previous guidelines, but for many, like myself, the habit of television viewing came long before the habit of conscious analysis; and television, like a primitive id, is part of some preintellectual psyche. But precisely because of its integral role in our unconscious lives, it is all the more crucial that television analysis be done by historians, now and in the future. It is time that television became a historical source, a critical document of our culture, and a prime-time endeavor.

The historian would seem to be particularly well prepared for this task. Trained to examine the remnant artifact as an expression of a much larger experience, to piece together fragments into a comprehensible whole, and to distill every ounce of significance from the apparently inconsequential, the historian brings an array of interpretive and analytic skills to television viewing. If he is any good, he will also bring an acid skepticism, the empiricist's hunger to know every available detail, and the Missourian's creed—show me. While the former inclinations push him to try to grasp the whole in the part through luxuriant theorizing, the latter provide him with the absolutely necessary restraints against a too rich fantasy. The historian knows that understanding demands both research and inspiration. But, as things now stand in television research and analysis, an understanding of television's role in our lives leans pretty heavily on inspiration. The historian, like the rest of the viewing public, is prone to an uncritical response which either claims too much (because TV is so omnipresent) or relegates television to an inconsequence which (if judged only by the quality of its content) seems to be just what it deserves. Neither approach, of course, gets us very far. And both, I suspect, result from the simple fact that television has, thus far, gone largely without the careful examination which the historian normally brings to his observations.

i

I would like, therefore, to try two things here: First, to apply to television programs certain traditional techniques of interpretive analysis with which most historians are familiar—techniques which tend to inflate the significance of television because they assume that TV is a significant part of our cultural equipment. And then, to pose some of the critical problems the historian will have to confront before he can hope to make these programs meaningful documents. Some of these problems are methodological, others are empirical and research-oriented, but both must be faced before inspiration can lead to a well-founded understanding. Of course, unanswered questions always present the pin to the bubble of grandiose claims and unexamined assumptions. This is just as it should be. I ask these questions not, however, to deny the significance of television or its usefulness. On the contrary, I ask them in order to stimulate the thought and research that will allow television to become a valuable part of the repertoire of our resources. Only as we begin to analyze and to question will the special problems of studying television emerge, and only then will the historian become aware (and wary) of both its promises and its problems.

I will begin with a content analysis of two television programs in order to demonstrate how common historical tools can help illuminate popular television themes and characters. The treatment I give these shows will necessarily be incomplete and less profound than I would like. A really solid analysis would take hundreds of hours of viewing, cross-references to other programs, careful attention to detail, and comparisons with other kinds of media sources like novels, movies, songs and advertisements. Since this is not possible here, I will limit myself to some general features of two programs, "The Mary Tyler Moore Show" and "M*A*S*H."

I have chosen these two because they are weekly programs, with continuing casts of characters, ongoing plots and themes, and maximum prime-time exposure. Both have been on the air for at least two seasons and both have been generally successful. They thus have the virtues of audience popularity, development over time, and thematic repetition, and they permit the historian to explore both changes and continuities in themes and images. Both are also (at least in my own estimation) amusing, entertaining, well-performed and produced. While I am not concerned with aesthetics here, I do think that the form critically affects content, and that in order to be an effective cultural mediator, a program must conform to certain common standards of craftsmanship and professionalism. "Mary Tyler Moore" and "M*A*S*H" conform to these standards.

ii

On its simplest level, "Mary Tyler Moore" is about a single girl on her own in a big city, away from family, home community, and conventional social bonds. She alone determines what she does, and she must depend on her work for self-support, her friends for comfort and companionship, and her good sense for survival. She does all three extremely well. Historians have long been accustomed to the many ways in which the theme of individualism has continued to agitate the cultural psyche, as Americans variously find their heroes on the frontier, in high political office, or in industrial entrepreneurship. Surely, here is the same theme in its modern guise—self-sufficiency, independence, personal virtue and courage. Mary has all of these qualities, but of course with a twist—a female twist. The American myth is lodged in masculine themes, the wilderness, the sea, the corporation, or the White House. This show draws on this background myth but substitutes a woman for a man.

Thus, "Mary Tyler Moore" is securely anchored in a persistent self-image of the culture. But it is also linked to the present through the specific sexual substitution and by the incorporation of present-day problems into that older framework. Mary is surely not "heroic" on the grand scale. She is no Carnegie, Lincoln or Crockett. Her heroism is of a personal and intimate variety and concerns her life rather than the nation's destiny. But it is a heroism which draws on the same virtues, individualism, resourcefulness and self-sufficiency, which connect her small-scale victories over adversity to theirs.

Mary's personal qualities are always the solid basis for most of the plots. She is loyal, hard-working, genuine, and sincere. Neither proud nor humble, she is attractive without being vain or glamorous. She is generous and warm, always hospitable, never cruel, and hardly ever angry without overwhelming cause. And she is profoundly sensible. (In one program, Mary readied to consume a huge breakfast with the self-conscious cliche, appreciated by the audience, that "breakfast is the most important meal of the day.") In short, Mary has character. Character in the American lexicon is more than personality. Personality makes life pleasant for others and Mary certainly does this. But character has the solidity and reliability which makes life good. This is the aura of the program.

Mary is also virtuous, but it is a modern virtue, attuned to evolving moral conventions. To be virtuous for a woman once meant to be chaste. Mary, at thirty-four, is hardly that, but neither is she promiscuous. More importantly, she neither flaunts her sex-love life, nor is obsessed by it. In fact, the best way to describe her sexual orientation may be negatively. Mary has no passion. This is as true in her dealings with co-workers as with her male friends. This is not to say that she has no commitment; quite the contrary. But passion is uncontrollable, and Mary's commitments are always directed, always controlled, always rationally informed.

Mary has charm without intensity. She survives without being pushy, succeeds without being domineering, can defend herself without aggressing. She may get angry, but she never gets hot. Certainly, in part, this reflects an ideal of modern woman with many links to the past. No longer sheltered or supported, she can make it on her own. No longer pure or innocent, she is still slightly repressed. Mary cannot possibly threaten men; she neither seduces them nor competes with them. (She alone still calls her boss "Mr. Grant.") I say this not as feminist criticism, but rather to suggest how older images have been adapted without doing violence to evolving sensibilities. Mary is neither mother nor whore, although she is both supportive and sexually attractive. She is a pal. (Something like Katherine Hepburn, without the acid biting edge.) That is the essence of the show's theme. Thus, part of the program's appeal is in the presentation of an alternative image for women. No longer locked into traditional categories, the show still never offends. It is a brilliant coup: Instead of painting modern women as men, or substituting pushy women for submissive women and loose women for chaste women, the show transcends traditional categories and emphasizes the core of the American image of virtue. Goodness is sundered from conventional sexual connotations. Mary is "good," not as a woman, but as a person. She is decent.

Recently the show has begun to play with more racy themes like adultery and explicit sexual involvement. But through all this, and in good part because Mary's character had been established before these themes were introduced, one can depend on Mary's good sense and decency. Mary remains fiercely jealous of her good name and intent on an unblemished personal reputation. But she can question traditional norms and proprieties because she has established her own solid, secure norm of implicit virtue and can draw on the ideals of her character. This succeeds so well precisely because the image of Mary has been permitted to develop over time (something only an ongoing medium like television can do). Mary's "goodness" can never really be questioned. Thus the show can adapt to new conventions without being dominated by them.* It has tapped the traditional reserve of American mythology and established a solid imagery of its own, and can therefore dabble in changing mores without being at the mercy of fashion. It incorporates new norms and is thus relevant without being faddish.

How this works in practice is best illustrated in the plot of a recent program. Mary's boss Lou is seeing a woman. This has transformed his outlook on life: He has donned new clothes (disapproved of but never criticized by Mary because they are merely modern without being attractive); he is taking unwonted cares about the office; he is cheerful and happy. The woman turns out to be a youngish, attractive, night-club singer and a woman "with a past" —three husbands and hardly veiled extramarital affairs. Mary finds

---

*"Mary Tyler Moore" has begun to respond to the feminist challenge: first on a program in which Mary demands that her salary be equal to that of her male (and better-paid) predecessor, and more recently when Mary was promoted from associate producer to producer. It is interesting that the first time Mary takes full control over a news production she becomes pushy, aggressive, and uncharacteristically angry and ill-tempered. In an illuminating remark, Betty White ("the happy homemaker") warns Mary that her ambition is wrecking her femininity. Of course, we can accept Mary's change of behavior because we have known her before and can rely on her implicit femininity as well as her more gentle nature. The accusation is a shibboleth and the program consciously turns it into this. This episode is a good illustration of how the history of the character's evolution (made possible by an ongoing medium) can permit the gradual incorporation of newer themes and still trust to the audience's sensibilities of the character's solidity.

her charming. She sees through the surface unconventionality to a solid, sterling and genuine person and approves immediately.

When the rest of the office staff finds out (Mary tells them, not realizing that others may find this woman contemptible), they are less charmed. They begin to make sly comments because they view Lou's friend according to traditional and conventional classifications of women. Lou, because he is still slave to conventional approbations and fearful of the opinions of his friends, retreats and gives up the affair. Mary is angered at this silly behavior, and accuses Lou of responding to outmoded ideas of propriety, rather than to his own sensibilities and evaluations. She points out that the woman's past is irrelevant and that he must judge her solely on the basis of his affections and her qualities of warmth, character, and kindness, not convention. In the funniest exchange of the program, Mary asks Lou how many sexual encounters establishes a woman as "that kind of woman." After a moment's thought, Lou answers "six." This one exchange turns all the conventional criteria of female virtue into a sham. Who, after all, can determine the precise line separating virtuous from nonvirtuous women during a period of changing sexual norms? It is really meaningless and ludicrous, and the brief exchange makes the point brilliantly.

Mary succeeds. Her good sense brings Lou to his own good sense, and he returns to his woman friend explaining that he was afraid that her greater sexual experience would make him feel insufficient. Lou has not entirely overcome his own qualms, however, for while he is willing to accept her sexual past, he still insists on counting only to five when she asks him how many men he thinks she has known. Lou has been able to save some conventional face, while accepting the more solid criteria of womanhood. Lou is still tied to convention. Mary, at least so far as her judgments of others are concerned, has completely transcended it.*

---

*This does not mean that Mary is not concerned with propriety in her own behavior. In one show, for example, she is brought close to tears by the spread of a bogus story Ted concocts about a love affair between them. In a confession in the office, she admits what we all know, that she cares deeply about what others think of her and fends off potential criticism by impeccable behavior. But Mary's horror at the story is grounded precisely in the fact that it is a lie, that she has done nothing to *deserve* the nasty rumors and the snickering innuendoes. Mary has been abused, not by an imputation of sexual behavior, but by sneaking and humiliating rumors. This is, of course, a variation on the theme of individualism, for she has been made to bear the unfair accusations about an action for which she bore no personal responsibility.

Television as a Cultural Force

This program can be explored from a host of interesting angles, not the least of which is the explicit reference to male anxieties about sexual performance in the context of female liberation. But the program is an outstanding example of the major thrust of the "Mary Tyler Moore" themes: Mary adjusts to modern changes without being overcome by them. She judges people by what they are, not whether they behave according to canons of shallow propriety. (This is especially true of her friendship with Rhoda.) Mary has good sense without being a goody-good in order to curry favor, and she has the faculty of independent judgment. Mary has the solid strength of character to be modern without being modish. Modern themes are touched lightly and with humor. They are used effectively because the program rests on solid human virtues linked to American myths and because these have been specifically developed during the life of the show itself.

Mary is not a deerslayer on the western frontier, but she is a woman alone on the urban frontier. Mary is an American folk hero at his or her best and the show is the very richest kind of source for cultural interpretation as it describes changing conventions in a rapidly changing society but provides evidence for the survival of those ideals and values solidified through a long history. Mary survives and succeeds because she embodies the characteristics of decency, sincerity, hard work, and fair play. Conventions change but Mary can survive because she adapts these qualities to the needs of a working woman in the modern world. I think the show's popularity is in no small measure due to the way in which it reaffirms values while it permits Mary to be up-to-date and modern. It is a comforting show. Like a shelter against the storm of change, it assures the audience that what is solid in the American character, male or female, will never be overpowered by fickle fashion.

An in-depth analysis of "Mary Tyler Moore" would go well beyond what I have merely skimmed over here and would, I believe, yield a rich vein of themes and characters. Each of the show's secondary characters draws on older American images: Lou is the practical boss, hard and vulgar on the outside, kind and sensitive on the inside; Rhoda is the ethnic without polish, but with freshness and vigor, enmeshed in a culture she cannot wholly assimilate but whose values obsess her (thinness, for example); Murray is the kindly co-worker, with literary aspirations, always beset by financial difficulties.

The show also introduces an important variation on the theme of modern individualism by supplementing it with the virtues of cooperation. First, the show always draws a distinction between Mary as a private person, alone, and Mary as a member of a news team. (She is found almost exclusively in two sets, at home and in the office.) Second, the show delicately balances the major theme of Mary's self-reliance and the modern realities of cooperation in the workplace. This is an important updating of earlier mythologies which described success almost exclusively as a function of individual exertion. Mary's personal qualities include cooperativeness, geniality, and kindness—all well tuned to the needs of group enterprise. It is well to remember that the fool of the show, Ted Baxter, is also an individualist, but in every way Mary's opposite, and that most of the mishaps at the station stem from his egotism, vainglory and insensitivity to group needs. Ted believes that he alone carries the whole burden of newscasting, and when he acts on that assumption he invariably upsets the applecart. Ted's failures are more than vanity, insensitivity and stinginess (all of which describe failure to relate to others). They result from his inability to cooperate and to adapt to the coordinate realities of the workplace. This critical feature of the show's "message" is just one illustration of how the program has realigned older themes to modern conditions.

But all the minor characters and themes can exist only because Mary is such a balanced character. She recognizes and brings out the best in others and handles difficult and ambiguous situations with judicious good sense. She is a stable center who unites all the characters into a common humanity. "The Mary Tyler Moore Show" is effective popular culture because it succeeds in incorporating American mythologies, the viewer's sympathies and a full array of modern social problems, with gentleness and humor. It is an expansive show, which connects universal aspirations of brotherhood and love, American traditions of fair play and individualism with present-day concerns. And it assures the viewer that problems can be resolved—through love, understanding, and good common sense.

iii

I would like to look more briefly at another show, "M*A*S*H." While "M*A*S*H" began as a movie and continues many of the general themes developed in a cinema medium, it has become an effective television program for some of the same reasons that sustain "Mary Tyler Moore"—the development of solid characters and the adaptation of traditional images to modern conditions. At the same time, it is more limited partly because it is locked into a time-frame, the Korean War, and because its materials are restricted to war and war-related themes. At its best, "M*A*S*H" transcends these limitations, as well as the brittle movie theme, by drawing on a broad American mythology, larger than war or army life.

"M*A*S*H" revolves around the adventures of two army buddies, a theme as rich in variations as the diverse literary imaginations of James Fenimore Cooper, Herman Melville, Mark Twain, and Ernest Hemingway could make it. It is a firm cultural axis for drawing on American ideals of loyalty, friendship, and humanitarian pluralism which vaunt the restrictions of convention and social structure. In "M*A*S*H," the rigid institutional bonds of army life which help to weld the friendship are at the same time a barrier which the intimate relationship must seek to overcome. Thus, as in many earlier renditions of the buddy theme, true friendship is created in a specific context, but the boundless claim of human relations battles with the encumbrances of social restriction.

In the most common "M*A*S*H" theme callow, pious and self-righteous patriotism, rigidly bound to bureaucratic procedure is juxtaposed with true, vital and sensitive loyalty. This is the source for most of the plots and the conscious basis for much of the humor. This juxtaposition is made all the more effective because it takes place within a medical setting where the urgency of saving human life is inhibited by formal, super-human rules and regulations. The bureaucracy, petty hierarchy, and inhibiting regulations of army life are surely premodern, and yet "M*A*S*H" can play on the viewer's sensitivity to these general conditions today where formal structures replace human values. The restrictions of the army thus serve as a kind of surrogate for all social norms which subordinate human needs, but are particularly cogent in terms of modern sensibilities.

There is a conscious primitivism in "M*A*S*H," an urge to make organic concerns like drink, sex, human relatedness, sometimes even childbirth, take precedence over the rules, norms and proprieties of civilization. In a recent program, for example, Hawkeye (shades of Cooper) Pierce (*Benjamin Franklin* Pierce, that American primitive original), and his pal Trapper (Cooper again) McIntyre risk their lives driving to an English medical unit to get a human artery for a surgical transplant that will save the leg of a soldier. The English commanding officer, fully uniformed like the proverbial imperialist in the jungle, is enjoying a well-set meal complete with wine in the midst of the human slaughter. He is completely impervious to the organic niceties of the operation, remarking only that his father had lost a leg in war and was splendidly content because it saved him the effort of fastening his shoe laces. The contrast between the ludicrous extreme of civilization represented by the British officer and the humanity of these vulgar American doctors, dashing madly for an artery, is dazzling. Civilization and its discontents has been reduced to the problem of shoe laces.

As a movie, "M*A*S*H" drew much of its black humor from effective cutting which contrasted scenes of gory bodies, the victims of mechanical warfare, with scenes of irreverent, usually sexual, play in the barracks. The television show can do less of this because it would be repugnant to the general audience, but also because the show has effectively deflected this irreverent, almost nihilistic humor into tamer and more liberal channels which balance primitivism and humanism. (The words to the movie theme, "Suicide is painless," but not the music, have been deleted on television.)

Captains Pierce and McIntyre are still interested in the good life, in martinis and nurses and golf, and they are spontaneous and alive. But, they also have a pointed commitment to humanitarian values (true medical ethics). Thus, they can deactivate a large bomb which threatens to explode in the camp, go to the rescue of American soldiers caught behind Red Chinese lines, treat Korean soldiers, or circumcise a mixed-blood infant—all at considerable risk to themselves—because their hedonism is tempered by ideals and liberal values. They are not ordered to do these things (indeed, the contrary is more frequently true). Rather, they act from spontaneous human sympathy, and because they embody the real American values which the war was purportedly fought to defend—democracy, brotherhood, and justice. Unlike officers like Frank Burns, they believe Koreans are human and should be treated fairly and with respect. On one program, Hawkeye breaks with a woman he is really thinking of marrying because she calls Koreans "gooks" and describes them as subhuman. Even Hawkeye's love for an individual cannot compete with his larger love for humankind. While the movie showed the inhumanity of war, the television program demonstrates that critical humanity (which is more than self-interest or spontaneous lust) can survive in any setting.

Television as a Cultural Force

Like Mary Tyler Moore, McIntyre and Pierce can disregard conventional conduct because they have solid virtues like personal honor and true loyalty. In contrast, Frank and Margaret (who represent the automatons of the organization) confuse loyalty with national chauvinism and use honor only as a substitute for personal ambition. "M*A*S*H" is purposely unconventional and "immoral" where "Mary Tyler Moore" is gently and only tangentially so. Yet both shows can do unconventional things because convention is not the issue. The sexual themes of "M*A*S*H" are more openly displayed and have been an integral part of the show from the first, but these too are subsumed to other human values like genuine affection and sensitivity. Where sex is merely passion as it is between Nurse Hoolihan and Captain Burns, it is crass, exploitative and evil. At worst, sex for McIntyre and Pierce is fun. It is unconventional but never uncontrollable as it frequently is with Margaret and Frank. Since Pierce is single, and McIntyre married, "M*A*S*H" has effectively turned all conventional criteria of sexual morality aside. Still, implicit goodness in sexual relationships is retained and there is a large difference between Burns' sexual exploitation, repressed behind a hypocritical facade of secrecy in the camp and a fierce resolve to maintain his marital relations ("civilized" sex), and Pierce and McIntyre's joyous primitive indulgence. Social conventions are flaunted; human ethics are not.

Despite the bucking of the rules and regulations of the institution, "M*A*S*H," like "Mary Tyler Moore," pays respectful deference to group cooperation. Loyalty is, however, defined in human terms. Pierce and McIntyre are both confirmed individualists who free themselves from conventions and proprieties, but they are bound to each other and are members of a larger team, both in the camp and in the operating room. Over the body of a patient, even the fierce antagonism between Pierce-McIntyre and Burns-Hoolihan melts away as they become fragments of a larger enterprise. Pierce and McIntyre resist being reduced to cogs in a military machine but recognize the implicit need for cooperation and personal adjustment in a humanitarian endeavor. There is a limit to individualism just as there is a limit to rigid institutional loyalty. "M*A*S*H" consciously ridicules hierarchy and subordination, and the camp is not governed by deferential salutes, hierarchical responsibilities (it is Corporal "Radar" O'Reilly, not Colonel Blake, who usually makes the decisions), or stern orders to inferiors, but by equalitarian camaraderie. Burns and Hoolihan can, of course, neither adapt to nor sanction the organization (or in their terms disorganization) of the camp because they conceive of the group as a bureaucratic calculator. Still, it is the group (democratically organized, to be sure, but still integrated) which makes personal survival and saving lives possible. Just as in "Mary Tyler Moore," successful work depends on coordinate endeavor.

Like "Mary Tyler Moore," "M*A*S*H" can play with up-to-date mores and new social realities because it incorporates them into an abiding context which is solid and humane. "M*A*S*H" is full of modern social themes—sexual freedom, racism, violence, bigotry. Its immediate appeal comes from the irreverent debunking of such outworn ideals as showy heroism, flashy patriotism, and crass materialism (especially effective because it plays on the economic motives of the American medical profession). Its strength comes from the fact that it contrasts these with more lasting human values. It opposes time-locked virtues and affirms transcendent human ideals like brotherhood and reverence for life. Thus "M*A*S*H" draws on American folk imagery of the unconventional man, strengthened through faithful friendship, in the service of a humanity larger than a specific country or people. American values have traditionally had this goal. The American democratic faith has, after all, always conceived of liberty, equality, and justice as fundamental and universal rights, and Americans have always assumed their institutions and ideals were an example to the world. "M*A*S*H" refurbishes these universalist aspirations. The irony, of course, is in the setting where the large goals are subsumed to parochial purposes and where the broader ideals of brotherhood and justice are forgotten in an often bigoted and selfish destruction of life. By drawing on these cultural values, "M*A*S*H" effectively anchors specific presentist concerns and mediates between the past and the present much as "Mary Tyler Moore" does. But where "Mary Tyler Moore" transcends traditional categories and judgments, "M*A*S*H" depends on the conscious rapid-fire denial of what is conventional, hypocritical and outworn. But both have sources deep in the American cultural past and link what is solid in that past with the specific problems of the day.

iv

In "M*A*S*H" and "Mary Tyler Moore," and in many other

programs, the historian can find a continuous thread of American imagery transposed and rejuvenated in a modern setting. I think that we can expect to find many old themes in this most modern of cultural transmitters. But, while television can provide the historian with a vast panorama of myths and values, he will have to do more than ask how the medium uses these older themes, what new ones are introduced, and how they are presented and juxtaposed. The historian must prepare to face a multitude of problems. With some of these he will already long be familiar, since they are part of the difficulties every historian has come to expect from his sources, those recalcitrant artifacts from which he tries to reconstruct living realities. Others will be new—implicit in the nature of the medium itself, in the relationship between the medium and its audience, and in the fact that television is a social agency as well as an interpreter of culture. The historian may well have to become fully acquainted with television technology, the art of serial screenwriting, and the peculiar habits of television viewing as well as the more traditional issues of editorial policy, economic control and government regulation, before he will be fully prepared to understand the significance of television in modern culture.

We will, I believe, have to meet television on its own turf before it can be fully enlisted into the historical ranks. But while many special problems will emerge as this initiation into a complex and technically aware television analysis takes place, there are some general issues which historians can prepare for as they grope their way toward a more refined understanding of the potentials and hazards of the medium for historical analysis. I would like to devote the rest of this paper to an examination of these from the perspective of a green historian, one who has barely gotten a foot in the water but already knows it to be deep.

In order to do so, it would be useful to first define and differentiate two features of television which historians will have to study before they can fully appreciate the historical uses of the medium. One of these is concerned with television as a structure, as a social and individual activity. The other concerns the content of television—the values, information and fantasies which television presents. Only as we know more about each can we begin to evaluate the role that television occupies in the culture and in the lives of its people.

Television is a modern institution and, as I suggested earlier, it is a fundamental experience, so habitual and regular that it must be compared with daily activities like meals, work or school. To assess the significance of this fact, historians will want to collect and evaluate data on the role of television in the society as a whole. We should know, for example, what part of the society's resources (human and monetary), are devoted to television, to advertising, media enterprises, the production and maintenance of receiving units. More critically, the historian will have to evaluate what role television viewing plays in the lives of individuals. How much time daily, weekly, or yearly do individuals spend viewing, when and with whom? It is essential that historians examine the implications of the home screen for the individual life, to see how it relates to family patterns, marital relations and child-rearing; how it integrates with other leisure pursuits like sports and reading; and finally how it affects personal patterns, eating habits, even attention span.

To understand the social life of modern man, the historian will have to come to terms with television viewing as an integral fact of that life. For just as the experience of work has been changed by the factory, the office, and the computer, so have personal habits, family, and leisure been affected by that plaything called television. It is an old cliche that the best way to watch television is with a beer can in one hand and the station tuner in the other. But this is not just a witty (and denigrating) remark; it is an extreme observation about social habits. Television is not only a regular experience. It is also an interrupted experience—interrupted by commercials, station breaks, public announcements, and not least by that itchy hand on the dial. These interruptions are part of its structure and they affect our sensibilities. In an odd way, our sensibilities have also been affected by the continuities of television. For television also creates connections in our lives as serials and weekly programs thread their way into our own interrupted lives and imaginations. Television has recreated human rhythms and, while historians cannot completely know how this affects psychology, they must at least consider how it relates to modern experience.

We should know or at least consider these things before we pretend to make intelligent sense of the content of television and its significance. The interpretation of content is, if anything, even more complex than an understanding of its structure for it is here that television poses all the old and many of the new problems of content analysis for the historian. Here again, distinctions are useful. Television programs can be broadly separated into two categories: news and entertainment.

Television as a Cultural Force

News programs, documentaries, white papers, election coverage, and interviews are meant to inform the public on political, social, and cultural issues. These are a recognizable fund of historical data, since they come so near what we ordinarily think of as "history." They will certainly become a basic source for historians as they try to untangle the knot of our time. The very fact of daily, immediate news programming is an important innovation in our social experience. Although my own interest is in the historical uses of television as entertainment rather than in its specific information, it may be well to remember that one of the complications of the medium is the tendency to obscure the differences between the two. In addition to all the problems which television news shares with other news sources (selection, bias and misrepresentation), other problems are specific to TV because news is engulfed in an entertainment medium. The structure of television tends to overwhelm distinctions between specific program content, and the interspersing of news with fun and fantasy erodes distinguishing sensibilities. Television news is, after all, a form of entertainment, just as nonserious programs are often a source of information. Nevertheless, there is some justice in distinguishing between the two. And it is the second of these forms, entertainment programs, with which I am most concerned.

Variety shows, situation comedies, television dramas, suspense and detective thrillers—these are the meat of prime-time programming and represent the largest part of the viewing public's fare. It is here that we must wrestle with TV as a cultural mediator as we confront the American popular imagination most intimately and most intensely. At home and in private, we face the American without his protective social garments. But while the potential historical returns are large because we come so near to common experience, the difficulties in the judicious use of these materials are equally so. I would like to focus on three of these difficulties implicit in all content analysis but exacerbated by the circumstances of the television medium: representation, control, and interpretation.

When the historian asks how representative a source is, he usually means how far it can be trusted to describe normal experience. That is, is it a genuine representative of the people he is studying, be they a whole society or a subgroup? He must beware that it is not anomalous or an artifact of the historical record. Thus, if he is using the *Atlantic Monthly* for the 1890s, the historian must be prepared to defend that magazine as an accurate gauge of American or American middle-class literary tastes, morality, and political views. He can cite circulation as a support for his contention, or he can suggest the similarity in the content with other magazines as an indication of general tendencies in the culture. Thus, both the size of the audience and the weight of the content measure the usefulness of the source. However, these factors are more difficult to determine in television, partly because of the facts of the medium and partly because representativeness is here manifestly related to the issue of control.

The modern historian has very few reliable estimates of a program's real popularity. The number of TV sets is no indication and while the Nielsen ratings do provide a certain measure of comparative popularity, they are not only vulnerable in their sampling techniques, but tell us little about the number of people watching, how long they watch, how much attention they pay. Many of these things we do not and possibly cannot know. Of course, we cannot know how many people who subscribed to the *Atlantic* normally read all or part of it either, but we can assume that, since buying is an active behavior, subscribers registered their intention to read the kinds of articles the *Atlantic* normally included. The editors of the *Atlantic* selected, at least in part, on the basis of their evaluation of this intended buying audience and its expectations. That audience is certainly much smaller than the total population and therefore more knowable. The same cannot be said of television. The audience for most commercial television programs is potentially the entire viewing public, all those who own or have access to a set. Ownership is certainly no indication of intent to watch a specific program or even a specific kind of program. And a rating may be deceptive. That a certain proportion of all sets are tuned to one program or another tells us only that one show is more or less popular than others available at that specific time. This may well indicate no more than viewers' intention to watch something rather than their interest in or genuine taste for a specific program.

The other bolster for judging the representativeness of a program, cross-reference of content (which relies on the weight of similar evidence), is less of an implicit problem in television. It is, however, aggravated by the issue of who controls the medium. Let me illustrate: If you wanted to see whether ethnicity was an important theme of television programming in the 1970s, you could reinforce first impressions gained from the repeated play on ethnic consciousness in "All In The Family," against other programs like "The Jeffersons," "Rhoda," "Barney Miller" or even "Sonny and

Cher." You would no doubt find substantial evidence that vague or specific ethnicity had become a common feature of programming. In this sphere, television is at least as conducive to substantiation by cross-referral of content as a literary source, because there is so much of it. But, another difficulty creeps in. Is ethnicity "big" on television because producers are pressured by consideration of equal opportunity, because sponsors are interested in reaching as wide an audience as possible, because directors and writers find ethnic stereotyping an easy substitute for characterization, or maybe just because it happened to work on one show and began to snowball in imitation? Probably you would be correct in asserting that there is some truth in each of these reasons and that ethnicity was certainly a hot issue on television in the seventies. That is itself extremely significant, of course, but it still does not answer what I think is the really crucial question of how much television reflects public sensibilities and to what degree it reflects the skewed sensibilities of the creators of television. What we want to understand, after all, is the public imagination.

Furthermore, this issue of media control subtly shades into a further complication—to what degree does the media create public sensibilities? This is certainly a problem in any popular medium which has normative and didactic as well as representational potential. The editor of the *Atlantic* may well be interested in instructing readers in how they should behave and think rather than in reflecting their views. All literary sources have this problem and historians are acutely aware of it. But it is a vastly more complicated problem in television, a national medium which reaches an unprecedented audience and where control is at once so centralized and so fragmented. The major broadcasters are a small fraternity who are drawn from the same class, work in the same region, respond to the same commercial interests, and are controlled by the same government agencies. At the same time, the inputs on even one program are vast; the program is the sum total of a congeries of individual personalities, tastes and biases. There are many cooks in the television kitchen and hordes at the table. Who determines what is to be consumed—advertisers, actors, producers, the FCC? And who sends the order—"middle America," New York, housewives, children? It is a complex, very complex mix.

But the problem is more complicated still. Ideally, the historian will want to know these things not for one program only, but for a sequence of programs which an individual watches during a day, a week or a year. This is hard enough to learn about a medium like the movies and vastly more difficult to determine about television. Television viewing is a pattern, not a single exposure. A truly significant statement about the content of television viewing would describe that pattern. But what are these sequences and how are they determined? Some "natural" sequences are predetermined by the medium. Such, for example, was the CBS Saturday night situation comedy lineup in 1974 which included "All In The Family," "M*A*S*H" or "The Jeffersons," "Mary Tyler Moore," and "Bob Newhart." But how many people (or which groups of people) would have switched the channels to get exactly this lineup? And how many actually do turn on specific programs on one night or different nights and what is this pattern? (One such pattern might be "Sanford and Son," "All In The Family," "Good Times," "Maude," and "Barney Miller"—different stations, different evenings, but all socially "relevant" in some way.) A fully matured content analysis of television viewing would concern itself not with one specific show or even with a series of the same shows, but with the overall pattern. That pattern may well reflect no more than the structure of television (that is, what is broadcast on a specific night on one channel or which competing programs are available at any one time or on a specific night). If this is so then historians must content themselves with observations about what an audience watches and not attempt grandiose hypotheses about the significance of their choices. I would hazard a guess, however, that this is not the case, and that a devotee of "M*A*S*H" does not watch "S.W.A.T."

It is all a very interactive mixture, made up of who controls, who determines, who selects, and finally, what it signifies. For, in television the issue of normative prescription is writ large. Daily exposure to television means that the views, the conventions, the sensibilities purveyed on the screen get not only maximum potential exposure but constant repetition, hourly, daily, weekly, yearly. If there was ever a vehicle which could create a public mind, this surely must be it. But does it? This is a difficult problem, no more easily determinable for the historian than the old conundrum of whether the young women exposed to the injunctions to chastity in nineteenth-century women's magazines remained chaste.

This leads me to the final problem historians must face in using television to understand the public and the culture—the problem of interpretation. Public symbols may have private meanings. One man watching "Mary Tyler Moore" may like her because she is a prude, another because she is liberated. The historian wishes to find in TV programs common interests, common values, and mediating cultural images so that he may penetrate the general social norms television captures and molds. But here we have the same difficulty any historian of culture faces, the problem of meaning. How do we know that the historian has not selected and dissected those things which interest him but may not be important to the general viewing public? Maybe the public couldn't care less whether Mary is old-fashioned or new-fangled, but likes her clothes or her voice. Selection is only one aspect of a more complex phenomenon. Symbols are complex; they connect many streams of feeling, personal histories and social norms. This is especially true in an ongoing medium. Because a TV program has a history of its own, it feeds on past experiences of the individual program and of the viewer, and each program is part of a larger pattern. It grows from an intricate network of inter-relationships and associations. How can the historian know these or the precise mix which makes one program more effective than another? How can he know whether an audience responds to the specific symbols of a single program, even if these can be determined, or whether that response is based on Mary's past experience, which a viewer has stored in his memory to be triggered by a convenient incident?

Television symbols of this kind are cumulative, and it is the particular hazard as well as the particular cogency of television as a popular culture medium that this is so. Television sets up a kind of connective tissue that ties the experiences of a program over time with the experiences of viewers over time. It is very difficult to untangle this web. At the same time, it can bring forth the richest vein of cultural experience. Because with television we have for the first time a new kind of cultural imagery, one that is not only locked into time, but has its own time sequence. As it crosses time as well as space, television imagery unites people and joins them in an ongoing experience. For the historian, television programs can do what very few other historical documents can: provide a focus for studying the slow process by which common images evolve within a recognizable context. At their best, television programs can at once stabilize public images and symbols and give them temporal elasticity. These are the most effective kinds of public symbols and the most useful as cultural documents because they parallel the historical process itself.

It is just this penetration into the shared and changing feature of the popular imagination for which television offers such a rich and promising avenue for historical analysis. But the historian must take infinite cares. He must select shows (patterns and sequences, if he can) which come closest to reflecting public aspirations, and he must attune himself to techniques of time analysis. He must, above all, penetrate into the web of private images specific to a show and the common images which connect that show with others and with the ongoing American sensibilities. But he can only do so with more information; information about television's structure, its part in the life of the individual, the family and the society; information about how decisions are made and who controls what goes on the air; information about viewing habits. Only then will he begin to understand just what it is that television tells us about an audience sitting at home with its hand on the dial.

The Bunkers,
the Critics
and the News

Kenneth M. Pierce

Boy the way Glenn Miller played
Songs that made the hit parade
Guys like us we had it made
Those were the days . . .

And you knew where you were then
Girls were girls and men were men
*Mister we could use a man like Herbert Hoover again . . . ***

The scene is familiar to millions of Americans: at 9:00 pm Monday night, Archie Bunker, a middle-aged man in shirt sleeves, and his wife Edith, who wears a faded house dress, sit at the piano in their living room. Unaware of the audience watching from the apparent distance of three feet, they sing—obviously a pair of amateurs, obviously having fun as they harmonize their song's big finale. Archie has been play-acting, imitating the popular crooners. He turns to his wife, punctuating his performance with a grand

---

Mr. Pierce has specialized in media studies while on the faculty of the University of Chicago, and, more recently, as editor of the *Columbia Journalism Review*.

*Used by permission. Lyrics by Lee Adams.

sweep of his cigar. Edith is gay but she doesn't catch his mood. She has banged artlessly at the piano; she does not notice now that Archie wants her approval. While she wonders what to do next, the television picture freezes, then dissolves.

It is a wonderful moment. Archie and Edith enjoy each other and themselves. They share a song and their memories, in private, at home. For a moment, television celebrates the pleasures of the hearth. And yet, this is not a simple celebration. Archie and Edith have wrapped their tenderness in a performance. They no longer know where they are, they sing. Nor do we know why they sing of the Depression days as happy days, an era when no help was needed from a "welfare state." Are the characters leveling with us? Shall we take their duet as a realistic moment or an artificial one? How are we to sort out the unusual combination here of intimacy, theatricality, nostalgia, and historical absurdity?

The popularity of "All In The Family" is an embarrassment to some critics—especially those who pledge their allegiance to standards of tolerance, liberalism, and good taste. They are in a bind because the head of the Bunker family seems a symbol of undesirable traits. His words and deeds mock enlightenment and compassion. Worse, his show has been accused of presenting wrongheaded actions and outlawed language only for commercial gain. Critics have thus invoked a dark view of the audience to explain the show's popularity (more than one-fifth of all Americans watched an average episode of "All In The Family" during 1974-75, the show's fourth season). Some have concluded that the audience is a large "booboisee," deficient in taste and ready to support (or unwilling to resist) intolerance and reaction.

It may be that the mass audience is perverse, but we ought to be skeptical when critics offer so extreme a conclusion, especially when they accompany their pleas for tolerance on television with their own intolerance for the audience. Once we realize that only the critic's failure to find merit in "All In The Family" leads him to postulate failings in the audience, we may reasonably wonder whether the critic, not the audience, is being perverse.

Critics are not like other members of the audience. They earn their living by discovering things to say about the media, and about life. They don't just sit before the TV set, they grapple with the programs. As they come to understand, they master what they see. What happens, though, when critics confront shows about—and for—

people who can't cope with the media? Perhaps they lack sympathy and understanding, for, as professionals, they find it hard to appreciate how easily the media can overwhelm people who are not critics.

"All In The Family" is a television series that usually takes for its subject the conflict of public, televised events with private, family life. It portrays a family that is a victim of this conflict, not its master. Archie and Edith are the opposite of modern critics (a term that can refer broadly to public men and women who devote themselves to mastering the flow of social novelty). Why such characters have recently become so popular is a very good question, but to answer it fully we will have to speculate about contemporary communication and culture. Some clues lie closer, in the way the shows are constructed, and it is to that subject that I turn first.

In any TV series, plots come and go each week. Unlike a single play or film, a TV series depends less on plot, more on whatever the many episodes have in common—usually characters and setting. The characters, not past events, are the "givens" in a series. Stories are designed to fit the characters, not *vice versa*, as in most other forms of drama.

This divorce of plot from character means that at least two kinds of series are possible. First, there is the series in which just about anything can happen, providing the action fits the general descriptions (age, sex, occupation and so forth) of the characters in their setting. Second, there is the series in which the characters are designed with a particular kind of story in mind.

The first kind of series is known as "situation comedy," if it is in a light vein. Such a series tends to give us types, not people, and to squeeze plots from the setting. (It is hard to squeeze plots out of types; types are malleable because they contain hardly any stuff.) "I Love Lucy" is a series of this kind. So is "The Mary Tyler Moore Show," which makes stories out of such events as a mother-in-law's visit to Mary's neighbor, or the accidents that almost prevent Mary from attending an award ceremony. Such situations yield plots for this series, but their resolutions tell us little about the characters. Anybody (or more precisely, nobody) does what is done each week. The series is strung together loosely, if at all, by the promise that these still-unknown people will do something amusing and warmhearted.

The second sort of series can be more absorbing, because

characters are more fully seen and incidents are more human when plot and character are connected. It is more interesting to watch a drama in which there is a close connection between who people are and what they do: then the story seems to reveal individual character, and individual traits of character have more to do with the development of the action. Stories with fully drawn characters cease to be contrivances, in other words, and become endowed with human significance. Yet, to the extent that a character is individualized, and to the extent that stories take account of that individuality, the adaptability of a character to many different stories decreases (of how many stories can Willy Loman, or Blanche DuBois, be hero?). This second kind of series, then, must strike a compromise between the type and the individual, between commonplace plots and plots that are special—between the series and the single drama. The compromise can be made, in a series of weekly stories, if the stories are alike in important ways. The use of plots that fit a pattern is an inevitable choice for a series that relies on the same characters, but seeks to individualize them.

During its five years on television, "All In The Family" has sometimes presented the more careless and cliched type of situation comedy. But for the most part, "All In The Family" has been that rare television series committed to a theme, to plots of a particular kind, and to characters who are defined by participation in the stories, and not merely by personality sketches in a script consultant's notebook.

Most of "All In The Family's" plots are based on issues that have recently agitated society. The story usually begins when something or somebody intrudes on the family, especially on its patriarch, Archie Bunker. A black family moves to the white neighborhood. A wife-swapping couple arrives at the Bunker home. A berserk computer informs Edith that it will pay the death benefit on Archie's life insurance. Edith suspects she has breast cancer. The Bunkers' daughter, Gloria, is mugged. Most of the stories develop comically, some do not, but all have as common theme the impact on the family of the world outside.

It is frequently observed that "All In The Family" deals, somehow, with social issues. But the plots tell us something more specific: issues impinge on the family, and the action in each show consists of the family's (or, sometimes, just Archie's) response. The Bunker family does not initiate—it reacts. And that reaction is the center of attention. The show's opening makes the point nicely: while Archie

62

and Edith sing their opening song, we look for a few seconds at things outside the home. First, we see the island of Manhattan, filmed from the air. Next, we are driving past a long row of homes in Queens. Soon just one home fills the screen, distinguished from the others only by the fact that the camera has stopped before it. These shots have had the artificial look of films on television. But then we come inside, very close to Edith and Archie; the videotape is clear and feels "live." This progression of closer views, and the switch from film to tape, tell us that this show is about the interplay between things inside and outside the home. And they take a stand: our frame of reference is inside.

The things outside this home are outside all of our homes, and they are generally brought inside by communications media, particularly television. However else they differ, the Bunkers and their audience share in a contemporary feast—of information (who is Margaux Hemingway? what is Cam Ranh Bay?), of social questions (where do I stand today on busing? detente? regulation of natural gas?) and of culture (what do I think of "The Godfather-Part II"? "Jaws"? *Fear of Flying*? *Watership Down*?). It is a safe bet that "All In The Family's" audience is reeling at the new horizons, new facts, and new values transmitted to all of us by television—in the news, the talk shows, and the dialogue of the entertainment shows.

This is an important clue to the appeal of the show. For the show's central theme is the confrontation between televised culture and the American family. This confrontation is a minor skirmish for those who—through necessity, habit, or education—have learned to make careful selections from the public agenda of those things to which they will attach private significance. But for those not in firm possession of devices for screening and selecting patterns of culture (for most of us, to varying degrees), the confrontation dramatized by "All In The Family" is constant and serious, with stakes including the way we see ourselves, our families, and our society.

We have already looked at this conflict in another guise: like TV series script writers, citizens are torn by the split of plot and character. They are searching for social patterns and self-definitions that will make it possible to link who they are, what they know and care about, and what they do. Television and other media are not the only forces that make such connection difficult. All sorts of divisions in modern life split character and plot (among them such divisions as office from home, education from employment, policy from execution).

But television and other media can have equally serious effects on our lives if we let them—and most of us do, to some extent. Character is eviscerated unless there is individual choice and experience; yet the media substitute public stereotypes for private experience. Plots are impossible without action; yet contemporary media quite literally put most people in the audience, divided from the actors on the stage. To the extent that we are dependent on the media, in other words, we may be in trouble. The people whose sets are turned on seven hours a day may not have the means to tell us about it (just as those who seldom watch television might find its effects difficult to imagine). But members of the Bunker family feel the impact of television; all one has to do is watch them.

Archie's chair faces the family television set. Television and movies are frequently discussed in this family, and they often provide subjects for opening business. In one episode, Archie wants to watch football, while his son-in-law Mike wants to watch a Jack Lemmon special on pollution. "You know what you can do with Jack Lemmon," Archie says. And Mike replies, "You know what you can do with John Wayne." Actually, neither of them can do anything with Jack Lemmon or John Wayne—except watch them.

But television is used for more than opening business. In another episode, Gloria returns home from a visit to her doctor, excited at the discovery that she is pregnant. Archie won't look up from "his" Knute Rockne movie to greet her and hear her news. Gloria must go to the kitchen to speak with her husband. "Guess what happened at the doctor's office," she says—and Mike begins to feel the panic that is conventionally ascribed to husbands in this situation. To buy time, Mike begins to talk like a television emcee: "Let's see, you found this purse with $300,000, right?" Gloria, put off by her father and now by her husband, complains:

"Why do things get turned around like this? I came home to tell you I'm going to have a baby and all of a sudden it's turned into a *whole other event*."

Whether we expect realism or entertaining fluff from the show, her outburst, remarkably, does not jar. The habits of television clowning and television watching lead Mike to distort and Archie to ignore Gloria's family news. It's as if she has lost control over her own drama—to television. Not a simple idea, but everyone understands her.

And then there is print. One evening a riddle occupies the family. Gloria says that her friend invented the riddle, and Edith thinks her friend must be very smart, because she thought up such a clever riddle. Archie disagrees: "Riddles ain't thought up. They come out of newspapers and magazines." This gag suggests that ordinary people lack creativity, and that newspapers are somehow disconnected from human beings.

Mike cites the newspapers in an argument about how to address the President, but Archie won't accept the example:

Archie: What are you writing to the President?
Mike: That's between Nixon and me.
Archie: "President" Nixon or "Mister" Nixon.
Mike: What's wrong with "Nixon"? The papers do it all the time.

In this pre-Watergate show, Archie follows Mike's example and writes his own letter to the president ("Richard E. Nixon," Archie calls him, incorrectly remembering the middle initial). Mike is writing to complain about pollution, ghettos, and war, and Archie decides that he will write a letter of thanks. As he struggles to compose a "proper" letter ("Dear Mr. President, your honor, sir . . ."), Archie dreams of the response his letter will receive. As the picture shimmers, Archie imagines that the President has chosen to respond personally, on television—and we see Archie, bathed in light, looking like nothing so much as the winner on a quiz show. A voice intones, to musical accompaniment:

"... In your President's opinion, Archie Bunker is (*CHORD*) one (*CHORD*) g-r-r-e-a-t (*CHORD*) American (*CLIMAX*)."

In the final scene of this show, Archie, Mike, and Edith return from the mailbox, dressed in their Sunday best, having just mailed the family's two letters to the President. They are silent, farcically struck by the solemnity of their act. Then, a doubt, and the mood returns to normal: they are not certain that anyone remembered to "jiggle" the mailbox after putting the letters in, and they rush outside to give the box a last "jiggle."

Some critics take Archie's (and Edith's) mispronunciations and other verbal confusions as a sign that the show patronizes its audience or makes fun of working people. But such errors are a result of the distance between this family and what is outside, between what is immediate or traditional and what is said on television: "Excitement to riot," "Harvey Belafonte," and "Richard E. Nixon." Yet Archie has no trouble with "Herbert Hoover." Nor does he bobble the names of people in the neighborhood or at work. It need not be a cheap gag (though it sometimes is) when Archie and Edith mix up names and phrases. Such mistakes are in character, and they help convey the show's theme. (I remember a woman living in one of Chicago's fashionable North Shore suburbs who explained to me, about a decade ago, that Strontium 90 was not so dangerous as other products of atomic tests because, as she had heard, "Strontium 90 only has a *half*-life." Such muddles are not restricted to any economic class, nor must they be taken today as rare occurrences. We are all, in this age of television and other forms of instant communication, forced to talk—if we wish to talk at all—of things about which we know very little.)

The children in this family are tuned in; their views, which they offer at the slightest provocation, seem formed by the news media. Mike and Gloria know about (and favor) such developments as daytime release of prison convicts, election of women to public office, and natural childbirth. Still, they don't know very much. For example, Mike's glib speech about the need for increases in social security payments sounds like what used to be called "book-learning," although its source is presumably television. There is no sign that Mike has thought about such complexities as the additional payroll deductions required to increase social security payments.

The members of this family differ in their receptivity to new information and new values. It is in these terms that the characters are given some individuality. The children are open to change. In fact, one suspects that there would be very little to their characters without the wealth of new signals which they have become adept at receiving.

Edith and Archie are out of touch, although to different degrees, and for different reasons. Edith is preoccupied with housework and tending to her family. Here she knows whereof she speaks. "The sweet rolls are ready," she worries before a Sunday breakfast, "and Archie hates it when the sugar drips." But as the conversation turns to other matters, she finds it hard to express herself and to understand others. In one episode, she plays solitaire while Archie talks, perking up after he mentions the "ace of spades":

> Edith: For goodness sake, Archie, you just said the ace of spades and I turned up the ace of spades—you see that in the movies and you say that wouldn't happen in real life but here we are in real life and it happened.
>
> Archie: (*After waiting for the end of this soliloquy*): We're in real life over here, Edith. Would you care to join us?

Edith's preoccupations and her lack of skill in receiving social clues lead her husband to call her a "dingbat," an insult—like so many others—that upsets her not at all. "Archie has a lot of sentiment," she explains to the children after he abandons her in a restaurant on her birthday, "you've just got to know where to look." Generally, she defers to Archie, brings him his beer, sympathizes at his lousy working day. The woman loves her family. She also excels in kindness, in putting herself in the place of another. Only once in about 25 shows have I seen her lose her temper: she got mad when Archie was thoughtlessly about to cause a workman to be fired. Because Archie was worried about the presence in his house of a well-meaning convict who was learning the plumbing trade, he decided to telephone the plumber's supervisor and ask him to take the man off the job. "Put down the phone," Edith twice asked Archie. And, when he refused, this gentle and blushing lady grabbed at the phone, and demanded: "*Goddamit*, put down the phone." Although Archie himself uses coarse language, he does not swear in front of women. Stunned by Edith's outburst, he obeyed, asking in a shocked rejoinder: "In front of the children?"

If only because she is so kind, and because her mind seems so nearly empty, Edith too is open to the new events, people, and words that bombard the home. Edith is "out of it," not "with it," but she has a strong sense of right and wrong, of duty to her immediate family, of concern for friends, relatives, and strangers. Secure in these, she mediates between her husband and the children, and between tradition and novelty.

Archie is different. The action that probably best expresses his character is his response, at election time, to a candidate for local office:

> Candidate: Excuse me, can I have a minute of your time?
>
> Archie: NO. (*Slams door in his face.*)

Archie is not committed to novelty, as are the kids. Nor is he open to novelty, as is Edith. He resists anything new, alien, outside. His home is not a castle, it is a barricade (perhaps it could be called a "bunker") from which he literally evicts wife-swappers, black neighbors, convicts, strangers, and uninvited relatives. But Archie also has other barricades. He uses derogatory names for "foreigners" —Americans of Italian, Spanish, and Jewish ancestry, and blacks. He does not wish to harm these and other strangers, he simply wishes to have nothing to do with them. An old man invited home by Edith makes Archie nervous, and leads him to dream that his children will mistreat him when he is old. Archie does not draw the obvious lesson from his dream: namely, that he would have less to worry about if he and everyone else treated old people better. Instead, Archie blames the old man for causing bad dreams, and renews his demands that Edith get the man out of his house. In another episode, Archie is stuck in an elevator while a woman gives birth, and he cannot bear to help, or even look at this uninvited scene. Rather than admit his paralysis to his family, he lies and tells them that he gave skillful assistance. Whether slamming his door, puffing out racial and ethnic slurs, or insulting his son-in-law ("meathead," he calls him), Archie is consistent. He wishes to put down, put off, or put away people and events which make him uncomfortable. And everything that he does not own or control, everything he does not understand, makes him uncomfortable.

Archie is rigidly self-centered. He can invoke "America" in order to defend himself, not the country. (Does Archie really wish to cheat a company, Edith asks? "Sure, that's the American way," he replies.) He can lie about his health to avoid joining his co-workers on a picket line. Neither Edith nor Archie are skilled in social graces, but while Edith always tries to do the proper thing (exchanging gifts, invitations, pleasantries), Archie shuns propriety. He cares little for what others think of him. Outsiders do not matter. Members of his family (at least his wife and daughter, if not his son-in-law) do matter, but, interestingly enough, he does not know how to express the affection he feels for them. The habit of shutting out and putting down is too strong. Gloria lies ill, at the end of one show, as Archie quietly and awkwardly enters her room:

Gloria: You want to say something, daddy?
Archie: No . . . (*pause*)
Gloria: You love me?

Kenneth M. Pierce

Archie: (*Nods in agreement*)
Gloria: I love you too, daddy.
            (*CLOSE UP OF ARCHIE, perhaps he is close
            to tears. Fade to black.*)

And again, in another show, Archie, drunk and afraid because he has locked himself in his own cellar, speaks a "last message" into a tape recorder:

"And Edith, a thing a guy usually don't tell a woman—
I love you."

Archie expects—and gets—little from his job. He does not register to vote (who cares about "meatball" elections, he asks). He cares little about most people. He is the local, self-centered member of this family, the one most intent on asserting and protecting his domain. The only insult that affected him, of the many he received in the shows I have seen, was an insult phrased in his own personal vocabulary: "My father had an expression to describe people like you, Mr. Bunker," says a friend brought home by the children, "You are a *meathead*." And indeed, his social and civic incompetence suggests that his retreat behind his barricade makes a kind of sense. Archie is determined to play the host when Sammy Davis, Jr. visits the Bunker home to retrieve a lost briefcase. Archie's interest in meeting a celebrity overcomes (but not completely) his aversion to blacks, just as the affection he feels for his family sometime overcomes his habitual distance and disdain. "Don't mention his eye," Archie twice warns Edith before the arrival of Davis, whose glass eye is occasionally discussed in gossip columns. Later, as Archie grandly pours coffee for Davis, he makes the slip: "Mr. Davis, do you take cream and sugar in your eye?"

As with other television shows, there are several ways to approach "All In The Family." We can talk about the show as a product of talent and skill, and try to describe how successfully the show does what it sets out to do, and the worth of that achievement. We can compare this series to other shows in the medium, as we did earlier. And we can enlarge the context to include the audience and the culture affected by television in general. In other words, our tasks are to name and appraise the effort, to describe the contribution made to its genre, and to account for the reaction of the audience. The first and last of these tasks remain to be completed.

Television as a Cultural Force

We've already said that each episode of "All In The Family" sets out to tell a story, that its characters are distinguished by their relation to "the news," and that the episodes portray the disruption of family life by social issues. Several things follow from this. The show is not designed to teach or propagandize; the intention here is story-telling, but it is pursued in this show with more consistency and care than is usual in situation comedies. No doubt people draw "messages" from the show, but the show is not designed to put across a message. It is no more to be blamed for the lessons its audience reads into it than are other more familiar kinds of fiction and drama. Archie Bunker is a bigot, it is said. Well, Iago was a murderer, but no one blames Shakespeare's *Othello* for that. Bonnie and Clyde were murderers and thieves. And further, Warren Beatty's movie aroused sympathy for them. Yet, it is not hard to defend this movie, since the sympathy aroused for the characters is part of a consistent and interesting effort to tell a story. The plot of this film centers on the way a pair of crooks came to inspire admiration and idol-worship. Given a plot, a story-telling purpose, such as this, it was necessary to present the murderers so as to produce sympathy and some admiration. We had to believe and to feel that crooks *could* become heroes, and the film showed their charm, while ignoring, until the end, the suffering they caused. Its subject was important and disturbing, the misdirection of our sympathies was an inevitable device, and the result was a good movie, albeit with evil characters.

Story-telling is like that. We don't have to welcome all the characters if they belong in the story. And I have attempted to show that "All In The Family," whatever its reputation among critics, has a consistent and interesting theme. In general (and with the exception of flaws to be noted shortly), this show has integrity. These characters belong in these plots. If this point has seldom been made in discussion of the show, that may be because we have been conditioned to talk about the people we see on television series as if they were people in our living rooms ("I like Mary Tyler Moore," or "Bob Newhart is so cute"), rather than as characters in stories. Or, perhaps, we have decided in advance that whatever is on television can't be serious. Perhaps *we* have become prejudiced, because television has so often disappointed us.

Considered as a series of short dramas, "All In The Family" is sometimes successful and sometimes not. When it works, it produces laughter, and affection and sympathy for the characters in their struggle with the larger world. But it is easy for the show to misfire, because these goals are contradictory: laughing at people can blot out our sympathy for them, and so can clumsy business that tries, but fails, to make us laugh. The best laughs in the show are gentle ones, consistent with the characters and in touch with the show's themes. Edith tells the children about a shared moment with Archie: "We both woke up together. We looked at each other, and I said, 'Good morning, Archie . . .' and he rolled over."

Unfortunately, forced gags are far more typical. Archie asks Edith to bring him an ice bag:

Edith: For your headache?
Archie: (*Annoyed*) No, I wanna build an igloo.

When our sympathy for the characters survives such bits, much of the credit is due Carroll O'Connor and Jean Stapleton, who play Archie and Edith. By extraordinary concentration on their roles, these gifted players manage to show us a love of family that is not always in the script. In fact, the entire series gains from unusual reliance on nonverbal devices—reactions, gestures, silence. The performances of O'Connor and Stapleton make the contortions of the scripts more believable than they would otherwise be, just as, in their opening song, these personalities create a credible and interesting episode, one that is independent of—and in spite of—the words they sing.

Cliches of social policy do not generate either laughter or sympathy for the characters, yet such cliches are uttered frequently during the show: an old man takes center stage to summarize the problems of old folks, or Sammy Davis, Jr. continues forever, it seems, to satirize Archie's bigotry. Propaganda for any view gets in the way in this show. Each episode has only a few minutes to convey a story, cause laughter, and create sympathy; the form is too limited to permit any interesting instruction about the world outside.

The worst episode I have seen fails because there is not only too much gag-writing, but the *shtick* aspires to profundity. This show presents the response of the family after Gloria is mugged (though not raped). Gloria must decide whether or not to report the incident to the police. Filing a complaint might protect other women, but it would increase Gloria's embarrassment and humiliation. The Bunkers decide not to report the incident. "I'm not responsible for all the other girls," Archie says.

It is not Gloria's selfish choice that leads me to consider this a bad show. There is much to be said for and against her choice. If the Bunker family is more cynical than my family about police work, and if they are less willing to heed the women's rights organizations who urge that women report such assaults, the choice is still in character, and an appropriate subject for drama.

What chiefly annoys in this show is the use of burlesque caricature to call forth a serious emotional response. We are asked to take seriously the agony of the family as it deliberates. But how can we care? Gloria makes her decision after a parade of bad gags about the evening dinner, and in response to a wiseacre caricature of the cross-examination she may face if she makes a complaint. It is as if Nora in *A Doll's House* made her painful decision by talking things over with Don Rickles or Jack E. Leonard; the attempt at anger and pity is botched by skimpy contrivance.

It is sometimes argued that "All In The Family" exploits social issues. Social issues may be given jarring treatment, but, if the description I have given of the characters and plots is accurate, it is not easy to find "exploitation" here. These outside issues are essential, not extraneous. They have changed the life of this family, and they are one side of the conflict that is played out in this show. The family attempts to maintain itself in the face of outside challenges. Take away the challenges and there is only equilibrium—Archie watching football, Mike studying, Edith cooking, Gloria helping. Not only are social issues used to get the story going, these issues and the media which bring them into this home are occasions for much of the Bunker's family life. Is there a family fight? Chances are it will be over which television show to watch, how fully Gloria cooperates with the police, how should the family respond to the presence of an old man?

The intrusion of all sorts of novel things (the title can be read *All* In The Family) helps make it clear that the Bunkers are, in many ways, admirably unfashionable. The family members care very much about their common existence as a family. Neither school, nor career, nor marriage has separated these children from these parents. Nor does social life or boredom force the Bunkers from their home. Archie and the children care enough about each other to fight out the generational conflicts; there are no agreements here to ignore each other, to neither hurt nor touch one another. Not a quiet place, not always a happy place, the Bunker home remains a place where things are shared, while two marriages and two generations remain together, despite all the changes and the threats outside.

The pleasures here for the audience are many and powerful. There is much about the show that is unrealistic, and yet the pleasure we feel in watching it is akin to recognition. Of course, the show is *acted*, explicitly put on for an audience. We can hear the laughter and applause. We see that the set has only three sides; the cameras are usually in front, where the audience sits. And, although they do not acknowledge it, Archie and Edith sing their opening song for our benefit—if only because they sing it the same way (it is the same tape) every week. This opening device is reminiscent of summer tent theatres, where the players often begin an evening's festivities with personal greetings, songs, and even the sale of lemonade. It serves the same purpose—winning our affection, sympathy, and attention for what is to follow.

Artificial, too, are the vaudeville and farce. For example, an undertaker, believing that Archie is dead, attempts to console Edith. When will she realize that the man has not stopped by to praise Archie, but to bury him? When will Archie return to the living room and greet the undertaker? Such dialogue and such scenes convince us that we are watching a show, not a slice of life. They emphasize the difference between the audience and the players: we are *watching* television, they are *on* television. And yet, when we see such ordinary, unremarkable things on television as giving the mailbox a "jiggle," there is the pleasure of recognition. These are things we consider of our family, things we have never before seen on television. There is also gratitude: television has, for a change, shown us things we know about. This effect is only possible because we usually feel there is a difference between what is on television and what is in our lives. It is a bit like watching the performance of a jazz musician and suddenly recognizing a phrase he quotes from a song we know. But, it is different, too, for in a nightclub or at a concert, we can applaud, and we know the performer will hear.

Television is intimate and personal, because it is in our homes, and because (if we watch it) it affects so much of our conversation and commands so much of our attention. It gives us an agenda that we are supposed to consider important. Yet television is strange. It deals not with our living room (though the set is there), but with things beyond—beyond our living room, beyond our family, and usually, beyond our community. Television's agenda cannot possibly include our own personal agenda of important things. Television is also impersonal, for its presentation is one-way; all we can do if we don't like its programs is turn them off—a gesture no more effective than Archie's attempt to push away outsiders by slamming his door. The gesture doesn't work. The Bunkers can't escape the news, and neither can we. Nor for that matter do we seem to be able to escape Johnny Carson, Margaux Hemingway, or Flip Wilson. The Bunkers talk to each other in the style of TV personalities, and so (often) do we.

It is not surprising that we delight at seeing things and people on television that are familiar to us but usually kept off the screen. The pleasure is one of triumph: the triumph of seeing things we know and value in the public forum. But "All In The Family" offers something more. It is the first series to recognize that the audience resents the power of television in their lives. Such resentment is inevitable, for television is a tease. It promises pleasure and knowledge, but only to the extent that we are willing to sit passively before it. Television surrounds us, but we can't touch or control it. We make television our supreme arbiter of status and importance, but it does not recognize us. And, as in the Bunker household, it aggravates the tensions between the generations. How can we not resent it?

In a sense, then, "All In The Family" gives the raspberry to television itself—primarily by showing things we usually consider private, things we have been taught are not permissible in public. When Archie says, "Cohen will win by a nose," we are not struck (or I am not struck) by anti-Semitism. Such cracks are heard among both Jews and Gentiles. Moreover, even when meant as insults, these remarks are "old hat." We are struck chiefly by the fact that such stuff is now on television. Something is being mocked here all right —but that something is not Jews (or any of the other subjects of Archie's invective). What is being mocked is the distance (in social class and status, in information and values, and simply in miles from the TV studio) that usually separates the performer from the audience, and what is public from what is private.

Many see Archie as the leader of a counter-revolution (even though he is the butt of the jokes) because he is an unrepentant victim of television's assault. Foreign cultures may decide the day, but nothing changes Archie, or his marriage, or the relationships within the Bunker family. Nor are the stories cast as victories for Edith or the kids. What happens is that this family (nothing fancy) persists, even as it absorbs the impact of television, and the families in the audience are grateful for an image of a family resisting (and succumbing to) television and things on television. Like graffiti,

"All In The Family" at once personalizes and subverts an institution that has taken power over us. And those of us in the under-class enjoy the ridicule of our overlords, even if we must thank them for it.

Television Melodrama

David Thorburn

I remember with what a smile of saying something daring and inacceptable John Erskine told an undergraduate class that some day we would understand that plot and melodrama were good things for a novel to have and that *Bleak House* was a very good novel indeed.

—Lionel Trilling,
A Gathering of Fugitives

Although much of what I say will touch significantly on the medium as a whole, I want to focus here on a single broad category of television programming—what *TV Guide* and the newspaper listings, with greater insight than they realize, designate as "melodrama." I believe that at its increasingly frequent best, this fundamental television genre so richly exploits the conventions of its medium as to be clearly distinguishable from its ancestors in the theater, in the novel,

Mr. Thorburn is Associate Professor of English at Yale University and the author of *Conrad's Romanticism* (1974). In 1975 he introduced a new course in the Yale curriculum concerned with popular narrative and television. During 1976-77, he will be working on a book about television with support from a grant from the American Council of Learned Societies.

and in films. And I also believe, though this more extravagant corollary judgment can only be implied in my present argument, that television melodrama has been our culture's most characteristic aesthetic form, and one of its most complex and serious forms as well, for at least the past decade and probably longer.

Melo is the Greek word for music. The term *melodrama* is said to have originated as a neutral designation for a spoken dramatic text with a musical accompaniment or background, an offshoot or spin-off of opera. The term came into widespread use in England during the nineteenth century, when it was appropriated by theatrical entrepreneurs as a legal device to circumvent statutes that restricted the performances of legitimate drama to certain theaters. In current popular and (much) learned usage, *melodrama* is a resolutely pejorative term, also originating early in the last century, denoting a sentimental, artificially plotted drama that sacrifices characterization to extravagant incident, makes sensational appeals to the emotions of its audience, and ends on a happy or at least a morally reassuring note.

Neither the older, neutral nor the current, disparaging definitions are remotely adequate, however. The best recent writings on melodrama, drawing sustenance from a larger body of work concerned with popular culture in general, have begun to articulate a far more complex definition, one that plausibly refuses to restrict melodrama to the theater, and vigorously challenges long-cherished distinctions between high and low culture—even going so far as to question some of our primary assumptions about the nature and possibilities of art itself. In this emerging conception, melodrama must be understood to include not only popular trash composed by hack novelists and film-makers—Conrad's forgotten rival Stanley Weyman, for example, Jacqueline Susann; the director Richard Fleischer—but also such complex, though still widely accessible, art-works as the novels of Samuel Richardson and Dickens, or the films of Hitchcock and Kurosawa. What is crucial to this new definition, though, is not the actual attributes of melodrama itself, which remain essentially unchanged; nor the extension of melodrama's claims to prose fiction and film, which many readers and viewers have long accepted in any case. What is crucial is the way in which the old dispraised attributes of melodrama are understood, the contexts to which they are returned, the respectful scrutiny they are assumed to deserve.[1]

What does it signify, for example, to acknowledge that the structure of melodrama enacts a fantasy of reassurance, and that the happy or moralistic endings so characteristic of the form are reductive and arbitrary—a denial of our "real" world where events refuse to be coherent and where (as Nabokov austerely says) harm is the norm? The desperate or cunning or spirited strategems by which this escape from reality is accomplished must still retain a fundamental interest. They must still instruct us, with whatever obliqueness, concerning the nature of that reality from which escape or respite has been sought. Consider the episode of the Cave of Montesinos in *Don Quixote*, in which the hero, no mean melodramatist himself, descends into a cavern to dream or conjure a pure vision of love and chivalry and returns with a tale in which a knight's heart is cut from his breast and salted to keep it fresh for his lady. This is an emblem, a crystallizing enactment, of the process whereby our freest, most necessary fantasies are anchored in the harsh, prosaic actualities of life. And Sancho's suspicious but also respectful and deeply attentive interrogation of Quixote's dream instructs us as to how we might profitably interrogate melodrama.

Again, consider the reassurance-structure of melodrama in relation to two other defining features of the form: its persistent and much-contemned habit of moral simplification and its lust for topicality, its hunger to engage or represent behavior and moral attitudes that belong to its particular day and time, especially behavior shocking or threatening to prevailing moral codes. When critics or viewers describe how television panders to its audience, these qualities of simplification and topicality are frequently cited in evidence. The audience wants to be titillated but also wants to be confirmed in its moral sloth, the argument goes, and so the melodramatist sells stories in which crime and criminals are absorbed into paradigms of moral conflict, into allegories of good and evil, in which the good almost always win. The trouble with such a view is not in what it describes, which is often accurate enough, but in its rush to judgment. Perhaps, as Roland Barthes proposes in his stunning essay on wrestling, we ought to learn to see such texts from the standpoint of the audience, whose pleasures in witnessing these spectacles of excess and grandiloquence may be deeper than we know, and whose intimate familiarity with such texts may lead them to perceive as complex aesthetic conventions what the traditional high culture sees only as simple stereotypes.[2]

Suppose that the reassuring conclusions and the moral allegorizing of melodrama are regarded in this way, as *conventions*, as "rules" of the genre in the same way that the iambic pentameter and the rimed couplet at the end of a sonnet are "rules" for that form. From this angle, these recurring features of melodrama can be perceived as the *enabling conditions* for an encounter with forbidden or deeply disturbing materials: not an escape into blindness or easy reassurance, but an instrument for seeing. And from this angle, melodrama becomes a peculiarly significant public forum, complicated and immensely enriched because its discourse is aesthetic and broadly popular: a forum or arena in which traditional ways of feeling and thinking are brought into continuous, strained relation with powerful intuitions of change and contingency.

This is the spirit in which I turn to television melodrama. In this category I include most made-for-television movies, the soap operas, and all the lawyers, cowboys, cops and docs, the fugitives and adventurers, the fraternal and filial comrades who have filled the prime hours of so many American nights for the last thirty years.[3] I have no wish to deny that these entertainments are market commodities first and last, imprisoned by rigid timetables and stereotyped formulas, compelled endlessly to imagine and reimagine as story and as performance the conventional wisdom, the lies and fantasies, and the muddled ambivalent values of our bourgeois industrial culture. These qualities are, in fact, the primary source of their interest for me, and of the complicated pleasures they uniquely offer.

Confined (but also nourished) by its own foreshortened history and by formal and thematic conventions whose origins are not so much aesthetic as economic, television melodrama is a derivative art, just now emerging from its infancy. It is effective more often in parts of stories than in their wholes, and in thrall to censoring pressures that limit its range. But like all true art, television melodrama is cunning, having discovered (or, more often, stumbled upon) strategies for using the constraints within which it must live.

Its essential artistic resource is the actor's performance, and one explanation—there are many others—for the disesteem in which television melodrama is held is that we have yet to articulate an adequate aesthetics for the art of performance. Far more decisively than the movie-actor, the television-actor creates and controls the meaning of what we see on the screen. In order to understand television drama, and in order to find authentic standards for judging it as art, we must learn to recognize and to value the discipline, energy, and intelligence that must be expended by the actor who succeeds in creating what we too casually call a *truthful* or *believable* performance. What happens when an actor's performance arouses our latent faculties of imaginative sympathy and moral judgment, when he causes us to acknowledge that what he is doing is true to the tangled potency of real experience, not simply impressive or clever, but *true*—what happens then is art.

It is important to be clear about what acting, especially television-acting, is or can be: nothing less than a reverent attentiveness to the pain and beauty in the lives of others, an attentiveness made accessible to us in a wonderfully instructive process wherein the performer's own impulses to self-assertion realize themselves only by surrendering or yielding to the claims of the character he wishes to portray. Richard Poirier, our best theorist of performance, puts the case as follows: "performance . . . is an action which must go through passages that both impede the action and give it form, much as a sculptor not only is impelled to shape his material but is in turn shaped by it, his impulse to mastery always chastened, sometimes made tender and possibly witty by the recalcitrance of what he is working on."[4]

Television has always challenged the actor. The medium's reduced visual scale grants him a primacy unavailable in the theater or in the movies, where an amplitude of things and spaces offers competition for the eye's attention. Its elaborate, enforced obedience to various formulas for plot and characterization virtually require him to recover from within himself and from his broadly stereotyped assignment nuances of gesture, inflection, and movement that will at least hint at individual or idiosyncratic qualities. And despite our failure clearly to acknowledge this, the history of television as a dramatic medium is, at the very least, a history of exceptional artistic accomplishment by actors. The performances in television melodrama today are much richer than in the past, though there were many remarkable performances even in the early days. The greater freedom afforded to writers and actors is part of the reason for this, but (as I will try to indicate shortly) the far more decisive reason is the extraordinary sophistication the genre has achieved.

Lacking access to even the most elementary scholarly resources —bibliographies, systematic collections of films or tapes, even moderately reliable histories of the art—I can only appeal to our (hopefully) common memory of the highly professional and serious acting regularly displayed in series such as "Naked City," "Twilight Zone," "Route 66," "Gunsmoke," "The Defenders," "Cade's County," "Stoney Burke," "East Side, West Side," "The Name of the Game," and others whose titles could be supplied by anyone who has watched American television over the past twenty or twenty-five years. Often the least promising dramatic formulas were transformed by vivid and highly intelligent performances. I remember with particular pleasure and respect, for example, Steve McQueen's arresting portrayal of the callow bounty hunter Josh Randall in the western series, "Wanted: Dead or Alive"—the jittery lean grace of his physical movements; the balked, dangerous tenderness registered by his voice and eyes in his encounters with women; the mingling of deference and menace that always enlivened his dealings with older men, outlaws and sheriffs mainly, between whom this memorable boy-hero seemed fixed or caught, but willingly so. McQueen's subsequent apotheosis in the movies was obviously deserved, but I have often felt his performances on the large screen were less tensely intelligent, more self-indulgent than his brilliant early work in television.

If we could free ourselves from our ingrained expectations concerning dramatic form and from our reluctance to acknowledge that art is always a commodity of some kind, constrained by the technology necessary to its production and by the needs of the audience for which it is intended, then we might begin to see how ingeniously television melodrama contrives to nourish its basic resource—the actor—even as it surrenders to those economic pressures that seem most imprisoning.

Consider, for example, the ubiquitous commercials. They are so widely deplored that even those who think themselves friendly to the medium cannot restrain their outrage over such unambiguous evidence of the huckster's contempt for art's claim to continuity. Thus, a writer in the official journal of the National Academy of Television Arts and Sciences, meditating sadly on "the total absence" of serious television drama, refers in passing to "the horrors of continuous, brutal interruption."[5]

That commercials have shaped television melodrama decisively is obvious, of course. But, as with most of the limitations to which the genre is subjected, these enforced pauses are merely formal conventions. They are no more intrinsically hostile to art than the unities observed by the French neoclassical theater or the serial installments in which so many Victorian novels had to be written. Their essential effect has been the refinement of a segmented dramatic structure peculiarly suited to a formula-story whose ending is predictable—the doctor will save the patient, the cop will catch the criminal—and whose capacity to surprise or otherwise engage its audience must therefore depend largely on the localized vividness and potency of the smaller units or episodes that comprise the whole.

Television melodrama achieves this episodic or segmented vividness in several ways, but its most dependable and recurring strategy is to require its actors to display themselves intensely and energetically from the very beginning. In its most characteristic and most interesting form, television melodrama will contrive its separate units such that they will have substantial independent weight and interest, usually enacting in miniature the larger patterns and emotional rhythms of the whole drama. Thus, each segment will show us a character, or several characters, confronting some difficulty or other; the character's behavior and (especially) his emotional responses will intensify, then achieve some sort of climactic or resolving pitch at the commercial break; and this pattern will be repeated incrementally in subsequent segments.

To describe this characteristic structure is to clarify what those who complain of the genre's improbability never acknowledge: that television melodrama is in some respects an *operatic* rather than a conventionally dramatic form—a fact openly indicated by the term *soap opera*. No one goes to Italian opera expecting a realistic plot, and since applause for the important arias is an inflexible convention, no one expects such works to proceed without interruption. The pleasures of this kind of opera are largely (though not exclusively) the pleasures of the brilliant individual performance, and good operas in this tradition are those in which the composer has contrived roles which test as fully as possible the vocal capacities of the performers.

Similarly, good television melodramas are those in which an intricately formulaic plot conspires perfectly with the commercial interruptions to encourage a rich articulation of the separate parts of the work, and thus to call forth from the realistic actor the full energies of his performer's gifts. What is implausible in such works is the continual necessity for emotional display by the characters. In real life we are rarely called upon to feel so intensely, and never in such neatly escalating sequences. But the emotions dramatized by these improbable plots are not in themselves unreal, or at least they need not be—and television melodrama often becomes more truthful as it becomes more implausible.

Television as a Cultural Force

As an example of this recurring paradox—it will be entirely familiar to any serious reader of Dickens—consider the following generically typical episode from the weekly series, "Medical Center." An active middle-aged man falls victim to an aneurysm judged certain to kill him within a few years. This affliction being strategically located for dramatic use, the operation that could save his life may also leave him impotent—a fate nasty enough for anyone, but psychologically debilitating for this unlucky fellow who has divorced his first wife and married a much younger woman. The early scenes establish his fear of aging and his intensely physical relationship with his young wife with fine lucid economy. Now the plot elaborates further complications and develops new, related centers of interest. His doctor—the series regular who is (sometimes) an arresting derivation of his television ancestors, Doctors Kildare and Ben Casey—is discovered to be a close, longtime friend whose involvement in the case is deeply personal. Confident of his surgeon's skills and much younger than his patient, the doctor is angrily unsympathetic to the older man's reluctance to save his life at the expense of his sexuality. Next, the rejected wife, brilliantly played by Barbara Rush, is introduced. She works—by a marvelous arbitrary coincidence—in the very hospital in which her ex-husband is being treated. There follows a complex scene in the hospital room in which the former wife acts out her tangled, deep feelings toward the man who has rejected her and toward the woman who has replaced her. In their tensely guarded repartee, the husband and ex-wife are shown to be bound to one another in a vulnerable knowingness made in decades of uneasy intimacy that no divorce can erase and that the new girl-wife must observe as an outsider. Later scenes require emotional confrontations—some of them equally subtle—between the doctor and each wife, between doctor and patient, between old wife and new.

These nearly mathematic symmetries conspire with still further plot complications to create a story that is implausible in the extreme. Though aneurysms are dangerous, they rarely threaten impotence. Though impotence is a real problem, few men are free to choose a short happy life of potency, and fewer still are surrounded in such crises by characters whose relations to them so fully articulate such a wide spectrum of human needs and attitudes. The test of such an arbitrary contrivance is not the plausibility of the whole but the accuracy and truthfulness of its parts, the extent to which its various strategies of artificial heightening permit an open enactment of feelings and desires that are only latent or diffused in the muddled incoherence of the real world. And although my argument does not depend on the success or failure of one or of one dozen specific melodramas—the genre's manifest complexity and its enormous popularity being sufficient to justify intensive and respectful study—I should say that the program just described was for me a serious aesthetic experience. I was caught by the persuasiveness of the actors' performances, and my sympathies were tested by the meanings those fine performances released. The credibility of the young wife's reluctant, pained acknowledgement that a life without sex *would* be a crippled life; the authenticity of the husband's partly childish, partly admirable reverence for his carnal aliveness; and, especially, the complex genuineness of his ambivalent continuing bonds with his first wife—all this was there on the screen. Far from falsifying life, it quickened one's awareness of the burdens and costs of human relationships.

That the plots of nearly all current television melodramas tend, as in this episode of "Medical Center," to be more artificially contrived than those of earlier years seems to me a measure not of the genre's unoriginality but of its maturity, its increasingly bold and self-conscious capacity to *use* formal requirements which it cannot in any case evade, and to exploit (rather than be exploited by) various formulas for characterization. Nearly all the better series melodramas of recent years, in fact, have resorted quite openly to what might be called a *multiplicity principle*: a principle of plotting or organization whereby a particular drama will draw not once or twice but many times upon the immense store of stories and situations created by the genre's brief but crowded history. The multiplicity principle allows not less but more reality to enter the genre. Where the old formulas had been developed exhaustively and singly through the whole of a story—that is how they became stereotypes—they are now treated elliptically in a plot that deploys many of them simultaneously. The familiar character-types and situations thus become more suggestive and less imprisoning. There is no pretense that a given character has been wholly "explained" by the plot, and the formula has the liberating effect of creating a premise or base on which the actor is free to build. By minimizing the need for long establishing or expository sequences, the multiplicity principle allows the story to leave aside the question of *how* these emotional entanglements were arrived at and to concentrate its energies on their credible and powerful present enactment.

These and other strategems—which result in richer, more plausible characterizations and also permit elegant variations of tone —are possible because television melodrama can rely confidently on one resource that is always essential to the vitality of any art-form: an audience impressive not simply in its numbers but also in its genuine sophistication, its deep familiarity with the history and conventions of the genre. For so literate an audience, the smallest departure from conventional expectations can become meaningful, and this creates endless chances for surprise and nuanced variation, even for thematic subtlety.

In his instructive book on American films of the '40s and '50s, Michael Wood speaks nostalgically of his membership in "the universal movie audience" of that time. This audience of tens of millions was able to see the movies as a coherent world, "a country of familiar faces, . . . a system of assumptions and beliefs and preoccupations, a fund of often interchangeable plots, characters, patches of dialog, and sets." By relying on the audience's familiarity with other movies, Wood says, the films of that era constituted "a living tradition of the kind that literary critics always used to be mourning for."[6]

This description fits contemporary television even more closely than it does those earlier movies, since most members of the TV audience have lived through the whole history of the medium. They know its habits, its formulas, its stars, and its recurring character actors with a confident, easy intimacy that may well be unique in the history of popular art. Moreover, television's capacity to make its history and evolution continuously available (even to younger members in its universal audience) is surely without precedent, for the system of reruns has now reached the point of transforming television into a continuous, living museum which displays for daily or weekly consumption texts from every stage of the medium's past.

Outsiders from the high culture who visit TV melodrama occasionally in order to issue their tedious reports about our cultural malaise are simply not seeing what the TV audience sees. They are especially blind to the complex allusiveness with which television melodrama uses its actors. For example, in a recent episode of the elegant "Columbo" series, Peter Falk's adventures occurred onboard a luxury liner and brought him into partnership with the captain of the ship, played by Patrick Macnee, the smooth British actor who starred in the popular spy series, "The Avengers." The scenes between Falk and Macnee were continuously enlivened not simply by the different acting styles of the two performers but also by the attitudes toward heroism, moral authority, and aesthetic taste represented in the kinds of programs with which each star has been associated. The uneasy, comic partnership between these characters —Falk's grungy, American-ethnic slyness contrasting with, and finally mocking, Macnee's British public school elegance and fastidiousness—was further complicated by the presence in the show of the guest villain, played by yet another star of a successful TV series of a few years ago—Robert Vaughn of "The Man From U.N.C.L.E." Vaughn's character had something of the sartorial, upper-class *elan* of Macnee's ship's master but, drawing on qualities established in his earlier TV role, was tougher, wholly American, more calculating, and ruthless. Macnee, of course, proved no match for Vaughn's unmannerly cunning, but Falk-Columbo succeeded in exposing him in a climax that expressed not only the show's usual fantasy of working-class intelligence overcoming aristocratic guile, but also the victory of American versions of popular entertainment over their British counterparts.

The aesthetic and human claims of most television melodrama would surely be much weakened, if not completely obliterated, in any other medium, and I have come to believe that the species of melodrama to be found on television today is a unique dramatic form, offering an especially persuasive resolution of the contradiction or tension that has been inherent in melodrama since the time of Euripides. As Peter Brooks reminds us in his provocative essay on the centrality of the melodramatic mode in romantic and modern culture, stage melodrama represents "a popular form of the tragic, exploiting similar emotions within the context of the ordinary." Melodrama is a "popular" form, we may say, both because it is favored by audiences and because it insists (or tries to insist) on the dignity and importance of the ordinary, usually bourgeois world of the theater-goer himself. The difficulty with this enterprise, of course, is the same for Arthur Miller in our own day as it was for Thomas Middleton in Jacobean London: displacing the action and characters from a mythic or heroically stylized world to an ordinary world—from Thebes to Brooklyn—involves a commitment to a kind of realism that is innately resistant to exactly those intense passionate enactments that the melodramatist wishes to invoke. Melodrama is thus always in conflict with itself, gesturing simultaneously toward ordinary reality *and* toward a moral and emotional heightening that is rarely encountered in the "real" world.

Although it can never be made to disappear, this conflict is minimized, or is capable of being minimized, by television—and in a way that is simply impossible in the live theater and that is nearly always less effective on the enlarged movie-screen. The melodramatic mode is peculiarly congenial to television, its inherent contradictions are less glaring and damaging there, because the medium is uniquely hospitable to the spatial confinements of the theater and to the profound realistic intimacy of the film.

Few would dispute the cinema's advantages over the theater as a realistic medium. As every serious film theorist begins by reminding us, the camera's ability to record the dense multiplicity of the external world and to reveal character in all its outer nuance and idiosyncrasy grants a visually authenticating power to the medium that has no equivalent in the theater. Though the stage owns advantages peculiar to its character as a live medium, it is clearly an artform more stylized, less visually realistic than the film, and it tests its performers in a somewhat different way. Perhaps the crucial difference is also the most obvious one: the distance between the audience and the actor in even the most intimate theatrical environment requires facial and vocal gestures as well as bodily movements "broader" and more excessive than those demanded by the camera, which can achieve a lover's closeness to the performer.

The cinema's photographic realism is not, of course, an unmixed blessing. But it is incalculably valuable to melodrama because, by encouraging understatement from its actors, it can help to ratify extravagant or intense emotions that would seem far less credible in the theater. And although television is the dwarf child of the film, constrained and scaled down in a great many ways, its very smallness can become an advantage to the melodramatic imagination. This is so because if the cinema's particularizing immediacy is friendly to melodrama, certain other characteristics of the medium are hostile to it. The extended duration of most film, the camera's freedom of movement, the more-than-life-sized dimensions of the cinematic image—all these create what has been called the film's mythopoeic tendency, its inevitable effect of magnification. Since the natural domain of melodrama is indoors, in those ordinary and enclosed spaces wherein most of us act out our deepest needs and feelings—bedrooms, offices, courtrooms, hospitals—the reduced visual field of television is, or can be, far more nourishing than the larger, naturally expansive movie-screen. And for the kind of psychologically nuanced performance elicited by good melodrama, the smaller television screen would seem even more appropriate: perfectly adapted, in fact, to record those intimately minute physical and vocal gestures on which the art of the realistic actor depends, yet happily free of the cinema's malicious (if often innocent) power to transform merely robust nostrils into Brobdingnagian caverns, minor facial irregularities into craterous deformities.

Television's matchless respect for the idiosyncratic expressiveness of the ordinary human face and its unique hospitality to the confining spaces of our ordinary world are virtues exploited repeatedly in all the better melodramas. But perhaps they are given special decisiveness in "Kojak," a classy police series whose gifted leading player had been previously consigned almost entirely to gangster parts, primarily (one supposes) because of the cinema's blindness to the uncosmetic beauty of his large bald head and generously irregular face. In its first two years particularly, before Savalas' character stiffened into the macho stereotype currently staring out upon us from magazine advertisements for razor blades and men's toiletries, "Kojak" was a genuine work of art, intricately designed to exploit its star's distinctively urban flamboyance, his gift for registering a long, modulated range of sarcastic vocal inflections and facial maneuvers, his talent for persuasive ranting. The show earned its general excellence not only because of Savalas' energetic performance, but also because its writers contrived supporting roles that complemented the central character with rare, individuating clarity, because the boldly artificial plotting in most episodes pressed toward the revelation of character rather than shoot-em-up action, and because, finally, the whole enterprise was forced into artfulness by the economic and technological environment that determined its life.

This last is at once the most decisive and most instructive fact about "Kojak," as it is about television melodrama generally. Because "Kojak" is filmed in Hollywood on a restricted budget, the show must invoke New York elliptically, in ingenious process shots and in stock footage taken from the full-length (and much less impressive) television-movie that served as a pilot for the series. The writers for the program are thus driven to devise stories that will allow the principal characters to appear in confined locations that can be created on or near studio sound-stages—offices; interrogation rooms, dingy bars, city apartments, nondescript alleys, highway underpasses, all the neutral and enclosed spaces common to urban life generally. As a result, "Kojak" often succeeds in projecting a sense of the city that is more compelling and intelligent than that which is offered in many films and television movies filmed on location: its menacing closeness, its capacity to harbor and even to generate certain kinds of crime, its watchful, unsettling accuracy as a custodian of the lists and records and documents that open a track to the very center of our lives. "Kojak's" clear superiority to another, ostensibly more original and exotic police series, "Hawaii Five-O," is good partial evidence for the liberating virtues of such confinement. This latter series is filmed on location at enormous expense and is often much concerned to give a flavor of Honolulu particularly. Yet it yields too easily to an obsession with scenic vistas and furious action sequences which threaten to transform the program into a mere travelogue and which always seem unnaturally confined by the reduced scale of the television screen.

That the characters in "Kojak" frequently press beyond the usual stereotypes is also partly a result of the show's inability to indulge in all the outdoor muscle-flexing, chasing, and shooting made possible by location filming. Savalas' Kojak especially is a richly individuated creation, his policeman's cunning a natural expression of his lifelong, intimate involvement in the very ecology of the city. A flamboyant, aggressive man, Kojak is continually engaged in a kind of joyful contest for recognition and even for mastery with the environment that surrounds him. The studio sets on which most of the action occurs, and the many close-up shots in each episode, reinforce and nurture these traits perfectly, for they help Savalas to work with real subtlety—to project not simply his character's impulse to define himself against the city's enclosures but also a wary, half-loving respect for such imprisonments, a sense indeed that they are the very instrument of his self-realization.

Kojak's expensive silk-lined suits and hats and the prancing vitality of his physical movements are merely the outer expressions of what is shown repeatedly to be an enterprise of personal fulfillment that depends mostly on force of intellect. His intelligence is not bookish—the son of a Greek immigrant, he never attended college—but it is genuine and powerfully self-defining because he must depend on his knowledge of the city in order to prevent a crime or catch a criminal. Proud of his superior mental quickness and urban knowingness, Kojak frequently behaves with the egotistical flair of a bold, demanding scholar, reveling in his ability to instruct subordinates in how many clues they have overlooked and even (in

90

one episode) performing with histrionic brilliance as a teacher before a class of students at the police academy. Objecting to this series because it ratifies the stereotype of the super-cop is as silly as objecting to Sherlock Holmes on similar grounds. Like Holmes in many ways, Kojak is a man who realizes deeply private needs and inclinations in the doing of his work. Not law-and-order simplicities, but intelligence and self-realization are what "Kojak" celebrates. The genius of the series is to have conceived a character whose portrayal calls forth from Savalas exactly what his appearance and talents most suit him to do.

The distinction of "Kojak" in its first two seasons seems to me reasonably representative of the achievements of television melodrama in recent years. During the past season, I have seen dozens of programs—episodes of "Harry-O," "Police Story," "Baretta," "Medical Center," the now-defunct "Medical Story," several made-for-TV movies, and portions at least of the new mini-series melodramas being developed by ABC—whose claims to attention were fully as strong as "Kojak's." Their partial but genuine excellence constitutes an especially salutary reminder of the fact that art always thrives on restraints and prohibitions, indeed that it requires them if it is to survive at all. Like the Renaissance sonnet or Racine's theater, television melodrama is always most successful when it most fully embraces that which confines it, when *all* the limitations imposed upon it—including such requirements as the 60 or 90-minute time slot, the commercial interruptions, the small dimensions of the screen, even the consequences of low-budget filming—become instruments of use, conventions whose combined workings create unpretentious and spirited dramatic entertainments, works of popular art that are engrossing, serious, and imaginative.

That such honorific adjectives are rarely applied to television melodrama, that we have effectively refused even to consider the genre in aesthetic terms is a cultural fact and, ultimately, a political fact almost as interesting as the art-works we have been ignoring. Perhaps because television melodrama is an authentically popular art—unlike rubber hamburgers, encounter-group theater or electric-kool-aid journalism—our understanding of it has been conditioned (if not thwarted entirely) by the enormous authority American high culture grants to avant-garde conceptions of the artist as an adversary figure in mortal conflict with his society. Our attitude toward the medium has been conditioned also by even more deeply ingrained assumptions about the separate high dignity of aesthetic experience—an activity we are schooled to imagine as uncontaminated by the marketplace, usually at enmity with the everyday world, and dignified by the very rituals of payment and dress and travel and isolation variously required for its enjoyment. It is hard, in an atmosphere which accords art a special if not an openly subversive status, to think of television as an aesthetic medium, for scarcely another institution in American life is at once so familiarly *un*-special and so profoundly a creature of the economic and technological genius of advanced industrial capitalism.

Almost everything that is said or written about television, and especially about television drama, is tainted by such prejudices; more often it is in utter servitude to them. And although television itself would no doubt benefit significantly if its nature were perceived and described more objectively, it is the larger culture—whose signature is daily and hourly to be found there—that would benefit far more.

In the introduction to *The Idea of a Theater*, Francis Fergusson reminds us that genuinely popular dramatic art is always powerfully conservative in certain ways, offering stories that insist on "their continuity with the common sense of the community." Hamlet could enjoin the players to hold a mirror up to nature, "to show . . . the very age and body of the time his form and pressure" because, Fergusson tells us, "the Elizabethan theater was itself a mirror which had been formed at the center of the culture of its time, and at the center of the life and awareness of the community." That we have no television Shakespeare is obvious enough, I guess. But we do already have our Thomas Kyds and our Chapmans. A Marlowe, even a Ben Jonson, is not inconceivable. It is time we noticed them.[7]

Footnotes

1. The bibliography of serious recent work on melodrama is not overly intimidating, but some exciting and important work has been done. I list here only pieces that have directly influenced my present argument, and I refer the reader to their notes and bibliographies for a fuller survey of the scholarship. Earl F. Bargainnier summarizes recent definitions of melodrama and offers a short history of the genre as practiced by dramatists of the eighteenth and nineteenth centuries in "Melodrama as Formula," *Journal of Popular Culture*, 9 (Winter, 1975). John G. Cawelti's indispensable *Adventure, Mystery, and Romance* (Chicago, 1976) focuses closely and originally on melodrama at several points. Peter Brooks' "The Melodramatic Imagination," in *Romanticism: Vistas, Instances, Continuities*, ed. David Thorburn and Geoffrey Hartman (Cornell, 1973), boldy argues that melodrama is a primary literary and visionary mode in romantic and modern culture. Much recent Dickens criticism is helpful on melodrama, but see especially Robert Garis, *The Dickens Theatre* (Oxford, 1965), and essays by Barbara Hardy, George H. Ford, and W. J. Harvey in the Dickens volume of the twentieth-century views series, ed. Martin Price (Prentice-Hall, 1967). Melodrama's complex, even symbiotic linkages with the economic and social institutions of capitalist democracy are a continuing (if implicit) theme of Ian Watt's classic *The Rise of the Novel* (University of California Press, 1957), and of Leo Braudy's remarkable essay on Richardson, "Penetration and Impenetrability in Clarissa," in *New Approaches to Eighteenth-Century Literature*, ed. Phillip Harth (Columbia University Press, 1974).

2. Roland Barthes, "The World of Wrestling," in *Mythologies*, trans. Annette Lavers (Hill and Wang, 1972). I am grateful to Jo Anne Lee of the University of California, Santa Barbara, for making me see the connection between Barthes' notions and television drama.

3. I will not discuss soap opera directly, partly because its serial nature differentiates it in certain respects from the prime-time shows, and also because this interesting subgenre of TV

melodrama has received some preliminary attention from others. See, for instance, Frederick L. Kaplan, "Intimacy and Conformity in American Soap Opera," *Journal of Popular Culture*, 9 (Winter, 1975); Renata Adler, "Afternoon Television: Unhappiness Enough and Time," *The New Yorker*, 47 (February 12, 1972); Marjorie Perloff, "Soap Bubbles," *The New Republic* (May 10, 1975); and the useful chapter on the soaps in Horace Newcomb's pioneering (if tentative) *TV, The Most Popular Art* (Anchor, 1974). Newcomb's book also contains sections on the prime-time shows I am calling melodramas. For an intelligent fan's impressions of soap opera, see Dan Wakefield's *All Her Children* (Doubleday, 1976).

4. Richard Poirier, *The Performing Self* (Oxford, 1971), p. xiv. I am deeply indebted to this crucial book, and to Poirier's later elaborations on his theory of performance in two pieces on ballet and another on Bette Midler (*The New Republic*, Janaury 5, 1974; March 15, 1975; August 2 & 9, 1975).

5. John Houseman, "TV Drama in the U.S.A.," *Television Quarterly*, 10 (Summer, 1973), p. 12.

6. Michael Wood, *America in the Movies* (Basic Books, 1975), pp. 10-11.

7. Though they are not to be held accountable for the uses to which I have put their advice, the following friends have read earlier versions of this essay and have saved me from many errors: Sheridan Blau, Leo Braudy, John Cawelti, Peter Clecak, Howard Felperin, Richard Slotkin, Alan Stephens, and Eugene Waith.

Media Medicine
and Morality

Robert S. Alley

A skeptic could reasonably argue that any questions one might pose concerning the social thrust and moral impact of television programming have already been answered by the very dominance of the profit motive in that industry. Certainly, producers must be economically successful in order to survive. However, those who populate the television industry, even the economic royalists, have other interests and goals in addition to the accumulation of wealth and power. A look at how this industry has treated the medical field reveals much about these additional interests and goals.

Historically, television has been cautious in its approach to medical science. Its first venture, called "Medic," was a well-received and highly realistic examination of surgery. The program sought to document medical case histories and used some actual hospital footage. This series began in 1954 and helped to launch the career of

Mr. Alley is chairman of the Department of Religion at the University of Richmond and is the author of two books. This essay will appear as a chapter in a forthcoming book by him on the subject of television and ethical values, to be published in the fall of 1976, and appears here with the permission of Abingdon Press.

Richard Boone who, after two years, moved to the lucrative and long-running "Have Gun, Will Travel." During its brief tenure, "Medic" was praised for its "seriousness and high-mindedness,"[1] even though Jack Gould of the *New York Times* felt it was sometimes marred by sensationalism. However, "Medic" came to an end at least partially because the portrayal of a Caesarean section was condemned before being shown by Father T. J. Flynn, director of radio and TV for the Roman Catholic Archdiocese of New York. This episode, entitled *The Glorious Red Gallagher*, was withdrawn by NBC after protest. General Electric and Procter and Gamble cancelled their sponsorship of the series, and the Los Angeles County Medical Association withdrew its endorsement. In May of 1956, the *Times* reported that NBC had decided to take "Medic" off the air.[2]

During the 1950s, medicine was a growth industry, a science, a pioneering profession seeking to provide better health and longer life—an extremely serious business. The adversary was disease and/or ignorance. Thus, "Medic" had attempted to convey information on such subjects as alcoholism, civil defense, and birth in a taut and intense manner, without humorous relief. Moreover, because the American public had been conditioned by a tense international political atmosphere, and was thinking cold war and brinksmanship, it was prepared to respond in dead earnest even to such trivial television fare as the one-dimensional dramas of the western genre: "Black Saddle," "Wyatt Earp," "Wanted: Dead or Alive," and "Gunsmoke." No wonder that realistic medical episodes were viewed with intensity.

After the demise of "Medic," no immediate medical successor appeared. During the 1960s, however, the Kennedy presidency provided a backdrop for a different perspective on the healing arts. In 1961, "Dr. Kildare" and "Ben Casey" appeared and created two significant cultural heroes. Both shows seemed intent upon capturing the efficiency, alertness, and dedication of youth, through the performances of Richard Chamberlain as Kildare and Vincent Edwards as Casey. Yet, both series also included the tempering influence of elder statesmen in the profession, portrayed by Raymond Massey (Dr. Gillespie) and Sam Jaffe (Dr. Zorba). A central theme seems to have been the "passing of the torch." The reasoned caution and compromise of the older generation were contrasted with the idealism of young surgeons, anxious to try new methods or champion unpopular causes. The setting of a metropolitan hospital for "Dr.

Kildare" provided the necessary variety of cases, most requiring surgery, even though the show's producer, David Victor, admits that a surgeon is not really involved daily in the lives of patients.

Since both series survived for five years and became immensely popular and lucrative for advertisers, some comparisons are in order. I have noticed in many hours of viewing over these past several years that ABC seems to be characterized by a certain coarseness of production which contrasts dramatically with the smoothness of NBC. For some curious reason that same comparison applies to the two characters, Casey and Kildare.

ABC's Casey was jarring, aggressive, a believer in justice. He consistently expressed anger, at times violently, and he "made waves." His sense of justice transcended the protocol of his profession. He was impatient. He quite often drew a line between the hard, long, underpaid hours of the hospital staff and profitable private practice. And, even as he was teaching doctors, he felt that dedication to principle (an important attribute to the younger generation in 1963) could force one to forego the pleasures of the medical good life.

NBC's Dr. Kildare, in contrast to Ben Casey, was cultured and refined. His education showed. He was respectful of authority. There was just the touch of piety in his demeanor not present in the abrupt righteousness of Casey. Yet, like Casey, Kildare often found just causes more important than surgical techniques and he was willing to challenge authority for such causes. Casey was an established professional and, as such, the writers tended to treat him as a static character with no ambition for advancement. Kildare, on the other hand, went from first year intern to chief resident, and thus exhibited growth incorporated in the plot. When Kildare's progress led producer David Victor to attempt to move him into private practice, NBC was not interested, because the network wished to retain a hospital setting. According to Victor, Marcus Welby "takes up a Dr. Kildare figure in the later years."[3]

The two programs inaugurated the idea of a plot in search of a disease. While "Medic" had focused upon the discipline of medicine, Kildare and Casey dwelt upon its practice. These two doctors, caught up in predictable dramatic structure, were heroic as they combatted the evils of death and ignorance. Since the adversary was inevitably impersonal, the pristine reputation of the medical practitioner was in no danger of becoming tarnished. The doctor/surgeon achieved heroic status for his participation in human conflicts through his expertise in the profession of medicine. The viewer identified this expertise by the use in the dialogue of technical jargon, effective "medical music," and masked faces but knowing glances.

Little, if any, understanding about illness and health was imparted to the lay public. As far as medical ethics were concerned, these were normally reduced to simplistic issues such as whether to inform a terminal patient of his or her condition. Such issues as medical incompetence, excessive fees, medical school quotas, euthanasia, abortion, birth control, and death with dignity were seldom addressed; and when they were, it was with a gingerly touch. Moreover, these early medical shows did not enjoy the freedom of language that prevails today. A good example is an episode of "Ben Casey" concerning a patient who was impotent. The word "impotent" could not be used, however, and the patient only alluded to his condition by such phrases as "I am not a real man." Had the word "impotent" been allowable in 1963, the script would have diminished by half.

Despite these limitations, medical shows made earlier attempts than other types of shows, such as police and lawyer series, to deal with personal drama. The reason for this was probably that public interest in a weekly bout with disease was limited. The result was that Casey and Kildare also became counselors and distributors of justice. They directed attention to humanistic values. Right was defined as standing for a patient against the system, or fighting bureaucratic red tape. Dr. Zorba and Dr. Gillespie were reminders of a gentler age of medicine, but an age no less conspicuous for its human concerns. Since Kildare and Casey were almost devoid of professional errors, their positions became nearly invulnerable.

Reflecting on his work in "Dr. Kildare," producer David Victor says that he believes his television drama "made a definite impact on the image of medicine." Richard Levinson and William Link, the producers and writers who presently have responsibility for "Columbo" and "Ellery Queen," have a different view. They believe that "popular entertainment does not create social change," but rather reinforces already held attitudes. These two men wrote an early "Dr. Kildare" script condemning funeral practices, "but as to whether it helped even one individual avoid exploitation at a time of bereavement we couldn't say. . . .All we can realistically hope for is to touch people aesthetically every now and then, and possibly, over a period of years, add an infinitesimal something to the prevailing climate of opinion."[4]

While a discussion of this matter would consume a chapter in itself, as a professor in the humanities who taught throughout the sixties, I am inclined to agree with Victor's judgment. The quality of idealism and optimism which grasped such a large portion of college students during that period could easily be attracted by the likes of Casey and Kildare. It was not that doctors were seen as holy and incapable of error. Rather, their potential for human service and unselfish utilization of the tools of medicine made the two TV doctors believable, if not typical. Yet, in the bitter years of 1965 through 1968, such idealism melted under the white heat of Vietnam. Both series disappeared after 1966, and three years passed before there was renewal of medical shows.

In some ways "The Bold Ones" was an effort to recapture the optimism which characterized the beginning of the decade by seeking the elusive "relevance" so prized in that era. This 1969 anthology dealt alternately with a white cop and a black district attorney, three law partners, a crusading senator, and a group of doctors. The doctors' portion of "The Bold Ones" helped revive medicine on television and, in so doing, attempted to engage "substantive issues" objectively, while "not taking a shot at anybody."[5] It also made a greater effort than previous shows to inform the audience about diseases and medical problems being treated. David Hartman, as Dr. Hunter, became a kind of teacher, and he recently commented to me that the series undertook to "use television to educate and inform while entertaining." On the other hand, while humor had gained slight entry in "Ben Casey" and "Dr. Kildare," it now came into full flower in the exchanges between Drs. Hunter and Stewart, with a quite believable senior medical officer played by E. G. Marshall.

Unfortunately, this ambitious undertaking collapsed in 1972, but not before it set some high standards for its genre. As an example, a 1972 drama, *Quality of Fear*, humanely engaged the critical issue of psychological treatment for cancer patients. Only in the privacy of a home setting could such a drama have a substantial impact. No other entertainment forum offers the same ideal conditions leading to significant intimate response.

"Marcus Welby, M.D.," the second long-running and highly popular medical show produced by David Victor, is a significant departure from previous medical shows in that it examines the work of two family physicians, Welby and Kiley. Before casting, Welby was drawn as a middle-aged man. However, when Robert Young was signed to play the part, the hero evolved into a compassionate senior general practitioner who largely reflects the personality of the star. Welby is a doctor who cares, who visits in homes, who is involved in patients' lives. Victor admits that Welby is "fictionalized, over-sentimentalized," but he believes "there *are* some Welbys." Indeed, admittedly for a diminishing portion of Americans, there are still doctors who are concerned with medicine as a healing art rather than as a means to a high standard of living.

Because of the nature of any dramatic series on TV, medical shows often assume a plurality of functions for the hero that may tend to suggest invincibility or even deification. Certainly this was true in the cases of Dr. Casey and Dr. Kildare. And, commenting on a "Welby" episode, student Elizabeth Gay wrote: "The plot is a fantasy, where doctors have time to case the streets for a patient. Superhumans, they not only hold the talisman of medical knowledge but have untold powers of persuasion and marriage counseling. They are superhuman in their devotion to others, they are always right and always know it." There are many who feel this medical glorification has exceeded sound judgment.

In a highly critical article entitled "The Great American Swash-bucklers," Peter Schrag asserts that "the deification of Medicine goes right on," and "for all their demystification of doctors, the new TV medical shows fail utterly to convey the idea that real health depends on confidence in self-management and the ability to cope."[6] It may be true that TV has failed to convey this idea, but then it is proper to ask whether the idea is valid. It would appear that Schrag has underestimated the depth of the prevailing, almost sacral character of medicine and healing which goes far beyond a simple and natural respect for a science that has helped to alleviate pain and suffering. From ancient times the medicine man has held a place of honor in society. Schrag's appeal to rationality alone overlooks the fact that, for most people today, medical science is still a very emotional and even mystic subject.

Yet medical shows are still basically vehicles for dramatic art—some good, some poor. They are part of the popular culture, utilizing the professions as artistic props. And the TV producer, because he lives in the realm of emotion as a script supervisor, usually desires to "deal with heroes not anti-heroes." His decision to have heroes determines the unrealistic, oversimplified issues and stereotypical characters often presented in these shows. Hopefully, as TV drama matures, other dimensions will find their way more often into new scripts.

The most moralistic TV doctor thus far has been Joe Gannon, the hero of "Medical Center," which was first aired in the same year as "Marcus Welby" and, like "Welby," is now in its sixth season. But, whereas Dr. Welby is a pragmatic traditionalist, Gannon is "hip." He is a modern matinee idol. Gannon is "cool." Teenagers, even younger children, make "Medical Center" a decided favorite in the Nielsen ratings.

Dr. Gannon champions causes in the name of openness. His is a "plea for tolerance of any deviation one can come up with"—for example, a friend who desires a transsexual operation. Actually, Gannon is a highly moral man who becomes angry when injustice appears in the plot. But his moral judgments are based on his acceptance of people as individuals and he resents those who seek to impose their own definitions on others.

Nevertheless, there are times when Gannon reveals that he has strong, predetermined attitudes about right and wrong, and, though he is less traditional than his rival, Dr. Welby, he is more doctrinaire. In an episode entitled *Aftershock*, Gannon remains committed to an absolute "pro-life" perspective and refuses to allow a terminal patient to die, even though the oxygen used by the dying man might deprive at least four healthy persons of the chance to survive. Gannon refuses, in his own words, to "play God." In some instances, Dr. Gannon seems to feel that it is murder not to employ every available means of life support. The notion that God decides upon the time of death is subtly woven into several scripts. Yet the fact that without modern technology and medicines, death would have occurred months or years earlier is apparently ignored. Gannon's perspective is not necessarily right, but proponents of alternate positions, such as "death with dignity," must still take his particular set of values into consideration.

In the 1969 episode *A Life In Waiting*, Gannon addresses the issue of abortion and expresses a profound belief in the "value of life." He moralizes heavily upon this theme as it relates to the unborn fetus and indicates that his students would laugh at his ideas. Yet, by the seventies, Gannon could champion the cause of a girl who wanted an abortion even when her parents were opposed to the idea. Obviously, a successful series must recognize cultural shifts and the need for change.[7]

In his capacity as producer for "Medical Center," Frank Glicksman looks for "subjects that are important, that have something to say." Now, after over 160 episodes of "Medical Center," he and his associate Don Brinkley feel that they are able to expose more of what is going on in the culture because America's youth are bringing more subjects to the surface. Special interest groups insist on being heard and, interestingly, Brinkley believes that pressure groups have forced the networks to deal with issues they would have previously buried under the rug.[8] As we noted with "Medic," pressure can operate both ways. However, the security against one point of view becoming dominant is the collaborative nature of the industry itself with its internal checks which tend to exclude excesses.

If the two current giants of the medical genre, "Marcus Welby, M.D." and "Medical Center," have a major common flaw, it may have to do with the neat, elegant, traditional, middle-class settings both present. If patients are from other than white middle- or upper-class environments their presence seems to require explanation. However, because the university setting of "Medical Center" is clearly upper middle-class, the clientele is certainly realistic. The same is true of Marcus Welby's practice. Perhaps Richard Levinson is right when he says that the "people who make TV only know upper-middle-class."

Women in these medical series are also represented in stereotyped ways. A recent content analysis of fifteen select shows found, at least in that limited sample, an overwhelming predominance of white male doctors and young white female nurses.[9] "Marcus Welby," for example, presents a rather traditional perspective on women. David Victor justifies this omission by pointing out that there was "no function for a wife in the series." Male dominance is presumed, reinforced by the receptionist Consuelo Lopez who carries the freight for the minority ethnic group while performing the "proper" womanly functions as a protective, emotional, and efficient employee. The current season has provided marriage for Dr. Kiley, a giant leap for TV physicians, but it has had little practical effect upon the plots.

The male dominance of the "Welby" program is gentle and paternalistic, but nevertheless, it is a clear-cut affirmation of the primary role of men in medicine. This is not to say that "Welby" is unusual in its treatment of women. Certainly, neither "Welby" nor "Medical Center" provide adequate professional models for women and girls who watch these shows. Even on the occasions when women are presented as full-fledged doctors, they have their special place.

In one memorable episode of "Ben Casey," Maggie, the female doctor, was portrayed as learning her place as a woman through counseling a patient:[10]

Female Patient: What can I do to help my husband?
Maggie: Let him [husband] make the decisions. Let him decide who your friends are.
Female Patient: That will change my whole way of life.
Maggie: Isn't that what getting married means?

Casey to Maggie concerning a date: What do you want to do?
Maggie: I'm not going to make that mistake. I'll do what you want to do.
Male doctor colleague: Who says doctors don't learn from their patients?

And it should also be noted that this treatment of women is not confined to television's medical programs. Women have little more than traditional roles on police and detective series. Angie Dickinson may be the star of "Police Woman," but she is essentially a weekly setup for male entrapment, a traditional female part. McMillan's wife is largely decorative; Columbo has an invisible but vocal Italian stereotype for a wife; Petrocelli's wife is a secretary. Most recently, "The Bionic Woman" has appeared as a "coequal" to "The Six Million Dollar Man," but she chooses to spend her time between adventures as—a schoolteacher!

At the same time, it is important to remember that this representation of women is a realistic one that does reflect things as they presently are. At a recent dental board hearing in Virginia (the entire State Board was male), a presentation in support of a controversial dental assistance program, nationally funded by the Department of Health, Education, and Welfare, included a slide presentation from HEW. The slides represented all dentists now and for the future as men, while most of the proposed dental assistants were women. Even HEW, when it is not thinking "women's rights," falls into long-held presumptions. In fact, Marcus Welby is more enlightened on this subject than many actual physicians seem to be. Though he resides in a traditional, picket fence world, he is a liberated man, accepting the new growth of independence and freedom for all persons.

But, does any of this really make any difference? Don't most people watch TV for entertainment and relaxation? Probably the answer is affirmative. Yet, as we are entertained, our minds do function. The reinforcement of values and principles in long-running shows surely must have impact. On this point, social scientists, network executives, writers, advertisers, producers, and humanists generally agree. Gannon and Welby, Casey and Kildare have reinforced some highly traditional values: honesty, trust, justice, freedom, tolerance, equality, education, family, hard work, discipline. Producer Richard Levinson, who would demur on any claim of permanent influence, does contend that conventional liberal attitudes have dominated television for the past fifteen years. Critic Michael Novak concurs: "We are lucky that the social class responsible for the creative side of television is not a reactionary and frankly illiberal class."[11] TV programs seem to conserve historically recognized, western ethical value structures within the context of "conventional" liberalism. For the present, given the oligopolistic capitalism in the three networks, and given our diverse political and religious affiliations, this may be a healthy compromise.

Of all the "values" considered by the medical programs, the question of trust may prove the most unsettling as it is portrayed in patient-doctor relationships. Patients are seldom represented as thinking rationally about their diseases. ("The Bold Ones" is an exception.) Instead, patients show irrational fear, misunderstanding, and resentment. No answer is provided to the question of how one may be assured that a particular doctor is worthy of trust. Pennsylvania Insurance Commissioner William Sheppard blamed " 'Marcus Welby' for causing the public to expect much more of doctors," and he claimed "the series might be one reason for an increase in malpractice suits."[12] Of course, being human, doctors do not measure up to their TV models, and the most recent forays into medical drama have attempted to cope with that matter.

NBC observed the marked success of its two competitors in the medical program field and decided to make two new entries into the 1975 ratings war. By the end of November, both "Medical Story" and "Doctors Hospital" were casualties of Nielsen. Despite critical acclaim, the former lost its place in the schedule.

In its first showing, NBC's "Medical Story" made a serious attempt to deal with malpractice and incompetence in the profession. In this episode, Dr. Ducker, an intern, struggles to prevent an operation by an established surgeon. He fails, as is illustrated in the following dialogue with the Chief Surgeon of Ducker's division in the hospital, a respected physician on the executive board:

Ducker: They are operating on Donnelly in the morning. (He explains the risks.)

Chief: What has this to do with me, Ducker?

Ducker: I'm going to ask you to put a call in to the Board.

Chief: It's not my case.

Ducker: But you verified my findings. I want you to call the Board.

Chief: You want me to call the Board or are you ordering me to?

Ducker: I'm sorry, sir. I don't know who to go to.

Chief: We can't have doctors interfering in other people's cases. It will cause chaos.

Ducker: I told you the symptoms, I told you what he [the surgeon] was doing. Are you saying you don't want to interfere because it would be bad form?

Chief: How do I know Dr. Nolan isn't right?

Ducker: I see. Yea! We are all members of the same club. There are certain things that we don't do even if a person's life is at stake.

Chief: I think you better go.

As it turns out, the operation does prove to be a mistake. The patient dies and the hospital Board has to admit that Dr. Nolan was wrong and Ducker was right. There follows a closing scene:

Chief: The Board is not going to renew your contract. It would cause too many tensions. . . .We are going to give you letters of recommendation. . . .This is an organization like anything else. Some things have to be sacrificed for larger things.

Ducker: What if I go to the papers? . . .the accrediting committee?

Chief: I wouldn't do that. You need your letters of recommendation. You'll find there is a tendency

>   to close ranks within the medical profession. If
>   you haven't learned anything else from this
>   episode you should have learned that.
> Ducker: I learned that.
> Chief: . . .you can't win.
> Ducker: All right I'm fired, but I'm still going to be a
>   doctor. . .

This anthology continued to investigate, on a weekly basis, such issues as the meaning of death with dignity, the use of patients as objects of experimentation, abortion, industrial poisoning, malpractice, and sterilization. There were still heroes, but they did not necessarily find success within the system. It was ironic to see Vincent Edwards (playing a new doctor, but with his old Ben Casey posture still unchanged) handcuffed by police and taken into custody for performing an alleged illegal abortion. This episode ends with the surgeon in question saying he will leave the matter in the hands of the court. And, venturing even further into the uncharted television territory, this episode portrays a priest as a "heavy." The words of Cleveland Amory seem appropriate: "Imagine a doctor show without a pat or a happy ending. We tell you it's a medical millenium."[13] Well, not exactly. The program was not popular and "Medical Story" fell to sixtieth place by late October. Despite brave predictions from NBC executives, economics dictated cancellation.

"Doctors Hospital" was more traditional than "Medical Story," but it suffered the same fate. George Peppard as a neurosurgeon reminded us of "Ben Casey." Yet there was an update. Like "Medical Story," this series gave sympathetic treatment to the role of women in medicine. There were flirtations with serious professional issues. In one particular episode, a woman surgeon is faced with the ultimate questions of life that finally tear at the presumption of medical diety. Then, out of a plethora of philosophizing reminiscent of Ecclesiastes, there emerges an essentially nontheistic humanism: "All there is is life and all that you can do is celebrate it."

The answer to why "Welby" and "Medical Center" survived, while two new competing efforts have failed, is not easily discovered. Familiarity certainly played a part. Competition in the allotted time slots is also an important consideration. However, I am inclined to believe that the TV medical show is historically in a distinct category. At no time since 1950 have more than three medical programs been simultaneously and successfully sustained. Yet the success which the industry has found in spin-offs and copies of other types of shows may have led executives and producers to expect the same principles to apply in the medical shows. I doubt that they do.

It is probable that the public reaches a saturation point in this area very quickly. For one thing, there is a strong viewer identification with the principal doctor characters of medical shows. Many supporters of one series tend to ignore other series. Part of the reason for this phenomenon may be that few of us consistently has more than one or two doctors attending us. Moreover, healing is an art with which we have frequent contact. Hospital visits are as common for most of us as prison and police station visits are rare. This surfeit of medicine in our personal lives may cause us to reject too much medicine on TV.

Also, another important reason for the failure of such a series as "Medical Story" may be that the public simply does not wish to have its trust in doctors challenged so directly. Viewers still seem more satisfied with medical shows which present familiar perspectives in health care and which tend to reinforce the already positive image of the doctor in society. The public's medical hero is a model of integrity, good citizenship, professionalism, and human kindness. And, on top of all these virtues, he is a believer in the ethic of hard work.

Medical shows which promote such super-doctors might easily convince one that the field of medicine is almost totally populated with professionals whose only commitment is to service. The economic rewards of the profession are not questioned, and one would scarcely guess that there are vast numbers of citizens living in poverty and discovering that their level of existence does not entitle them to receive the medical services which their TV sets promise them.

However distorted this altogether positive image of medical professionals as a whole may be, it is easy to understand that it is an accurate reflection of society's *desires*. People still want to believe in their doctors. The vast majority of seriously ill patients still want to believe that, "if there is a cure," then their doctor will find the surgeons or other specialists to attack the disease. Because the ultimate concerns of these medical shows—the mysteries of life, sickness, and death—are profound, attitudes about them change slowly, and the history of the genre suggests that successful programs cannot differ greatly from the prevailing attitudes and beliefs of their audience.

Yet a few successful shows *have* given attention to the critical issues of medical ethics—malpractice, euthanasia, genetics, fee structures, hospital costs. During its brief tenure, "Medical Story" opened many of these issues for viewing and challenged the mythic image of doctors. For instance, "Medical Story" raised the suspicion that one's doctor might not know "the cure" and that, if he did, his personal character could affect the outcome of the case as significantly as the procedure he chose to use. Despite the fact that "Medical Story" met an untimely death, its presence on NBC for almost four months points to a qualitative leap in the treatment of medical drama.

Of course, the medical dramas intend to entertain, and it is within this frame of reference that discussion of impact must occur. But current medical dramas also show every intention of including moral and ethical comment as well—a motive which is certainly not antithetical to good entertainment. Although traditionalism remains a strong element in most medical series, there *are* messages being delivered. There are also challenges to modern medical practices, and a few more realistic medical models. This continuing struggle over humanistic values portrayed on the tube may have a salutary effect on viewers, and some producers in the television industry believe that there are still ways to develop greater maturity in TV medicine.

That there is a connection between television's medical shows and societal conditions seems clear. However, which has the greater influence on the other is less clear. Are we being conditioned, or are we merely viewing reflections of ourselves and our culture on TV? Probably there is some of both. Yet the public is showing increased interest in the issues of medical science, as the Quinlan euthanasia controversy verifies. And if it is true, as recent disclosures in nationally published inquiries suggest, that five percent of practicing physicians are incompetent,[14] then the possibility that doctor shows are causing more malpractice suits may be an encouraging sign. Hopefully, greater expectations will produce more responsible doctors. In any case, whether they are a cause or effect in society, television's medical shows are a unique and significant forum for public consideration of questions which literally are matters of life and death.

Chronology of Primetime Medical Programs

	1954 '55 '56 '57 '58 '59 '60 '61 '62 '63 '64 '65 '66 '67 '68 '69 '70 '71 '72 '73 '74 '75
Medic Ben Casey	
Dr. Kildare The Bold Ones	
Marcus Welby, M.D.** Medical Center*	
Medical Story** Doctors' Hospital**	

* Continuing Shows
** Cancelled Shows

Footnotes

1. *New York Times*, September 15, 1954, 48:3.

2. *New York Times*, May 25, 1956, 47:5.

3. I wish to thank David Victor for an interview in July of 1975 and other assistance rendered by Norman Fox.

4. I express appreciation to Richard Levinson and William Link for a lengthy interview held in July, 1975. Quotations are from that session and from other materials supplied by them.

5. David Hartman kindly submitted to two interviews, July and December, 1975. He also made available a most useful tape and arranged several meetings for me while I was in Los Angeles.

6. Peter Schrag. "The Great American Swashbucklers," *More*, November, 1975.

7. By contrast, in a 1972 episode on abortion, Dr. Welby approaches this issue neither moralistically nor legalistically. For the pragmatic Marcus Welby, the welfare of his patient and her psychological state determines his decision. He can express respect for the attitudes of the girl's parents, while deploring "parental tyranny."

8. The help extended by Frank Glicksman has been useful and much appreciated. He and Don Brinkley spent the better part of one afternoon in July, 1975, discussing with me their work. In addition, I have received numerous "Medical Center" scripts for information purposes.

9. James M. McLaughlin. "Characteristics and Symbolic Functions of Fictional Televised Medical Professionals and Their Effect on Children," unpublished M.A. dissertation, The Annenberg School of Communications, The University of Pennsylvania, 1975, p. 10. (This research did not include the most recent programs, "Medical Center" and "Doctors Hospital.")

10. All dialogue contained in this essay was taken from programs at the time of airing.

11. Michael Novak. "Television Shapes the Soul," *Television as a Social Force: New Approaches to TV Criticism*, Praeger Publishers, N.Y., 1975, p. 21.

12. McLaughlin, *op. cit.*, p. 36.

13. Cleveland Amory. "Review," *TV Guide*, Vol. 23, No. 44, November 1, 1975, p. 20.

14. *New York Times*, January 26, 1976, 1:1.

Television as
a Moral Educator

Kevin Ryan

The influence of television on public morality is one of those perennially "hot" topics which can ignite a dull cocktail party or attract attention to a newspaper's editorial page. Yet, by and large, what TV is doing to us is still a mystery. It's new. We know that television is a complex experience which takes up a great deal of our lives, but we find it difficult to gauge its impact.

So, when we join the cloudy issues of morality with the mysteries of television, we bring together two human concerns about which much is felt, but relatively little is known. The adult community is traditionally concerned with passing on its values to the young. Increased crime rates, revelations of corruption in our highest governmental offices, rapid change in sexual mores and marital patterns, and an apparent descent from personal honesty have all deepened this concern and sent people looking for the causes of this overall decline in morality. The presence of television is an obvious difference between the childhood environment of today's adult and that of today's youth. We are told that children now spend more time before the television tube than in the classroom. While some

---

Mr. Ryan is Associate Dean in the College of Education at the Ohio State University. In the last ten years, he has taught on the faculties of Stanford, Harvard and the University of Chicago.

insist that there is no evidence of a causal link between the rise in consumption of TV and the rise of delinquency, it is all but irresistible not to point out a correlation.

Those who would have us believe there is a relationship between television consumption and immoral behavior often argue as follows: from Saturday-morning cartoons to prime-time adventures, TV parades before the young an unrelenting series of antisocial heroes and villains. During their most impressionable years, children are exposed to these models of immoral and often vicious behavior. Thus, the civil and moral values of the home are eroded while the children sit quietly glued to the tube in the den.

Moreover, in its quest to capture public attention, television fills key viewing times with violent words, hostile acts, and capricious shootings and killings. This type of behavior is so common on television that, for the young, the value of life is cheapened and debased. The most horrible of acts, the taking of human life, is so common on television that murder loses its meaning for the street punk. Neat, sterilized slayings on television remove the full impact of this most heinous crime.

The *Chicago Tribune* has reported that a six-year veteran of the homicide squad, Detective DiLeonardi, counted thirteen deaths on television during prime-time in one evening. Apparently DiLeonardi is convinced that there is a direct relationship between violent crime and the media. For the last year and a half, he has been recording the number of TV violent deaths. Currently, his count is over 1,300. The *Chicago Tribune* seems to have joined Detective DiLeonardi's campaign.

Recently I did a survey of a thousand educators on the role of the school and other agencies in moral education.[1] While these educators see the home, the church, and the school as having a strong positive impact on the moral development of the young, they see mass media (the most obvious of which I believe is television) as having a pernicious effect on the moral life of children. When asked about the potential of various institutions, only twenty-seven percent thought that the mass media might be an effective and positive moral educator while fully sixty-four percent of the respondents viewed the mass media as having a negative effect on children.

Despite these arguments against television, a contrasting view sees TV as a much-needed prop to falling public morality. The impact of religion on morality has been severely weakened. Public schools for the last two decades have given serious moral issues a wide berth. Teachers are just as confused about moral issues as the rest of the public. The family, another weakened institution, has less hold on children and is less effective in transferring positive values. Television, on the other hand, has become the new and forceful purveyor of moral values, according to this point of view. Although certainly the "Mary Tyler Moore"-"All In The Family" situation comedy shows give middle-class standards of behavior strong support, it is the adventure stories—the police and medical adventures and the westerns—that really reveal the essential morality of TV. Transgressors are always punished. The good, clearly identified, are normally vindicated and are always subjects of our admiration. Those who would violate the common good or the accepted standards of morality are portrayed as evil, or, alas, maladjusted. Public morality is rarely violated by the happy, well-adjusted man or woman.

This theory of television as the supporter of middle-class values was reiterated by Michael J. Arlen in the April 21 *New Yorker*. Arlen was grieving about the denuded simplicity and predictability of TV adventures. He stated that we always know that the heroes will triumph and good will overcome. Therefore, TV is essentially insincere. He laments that our TV shows have none of the mythic power of the *Iliad*, *King Lear*, and other great works of our literary tradition. He sees Kojak, Mannix and Captain Kirk not as mythic heroes, but rather as the "dying embers of a 19th century pietistic morality." He would go further than most and assert that TV is not merely morally benign, but morally banal. "No matter how much killing and shooting takes place in a detective or western program, the one note that seems to reverberate through the action is the moral position of the detective or sheriff—and the moral position of the program—our storyteller."

The Cognitive-Developmental
Approach to Moral Development

The issue of the impact of television on morality has not been settled by philosophical analysis or empirical studies. We are still left with the question of what effect all this television has on the young. How, if at all, do these real and fictionalized reflections of the human condition affect the subsequent behavior of the young viewer?

Troubled parents and educators have no answer to this pressing question. However, there has recently emerged a theory of how children develop in their capacity for moral thought. Although this theory cannot directly explain what TV is actually doing to the morals and moral thinking of our young, it could provide a tool for understanding what and how television is communicating to us in the moral realm. This comprehensive and elegant theory of moral development has been formulated by Lawrence Kohlberg of Harvard University and is referred to as the Cognitive-Developmental Approach to Moral Development. Taking off from Jean Piaget's earlier work in moral development, Kohlberg has done a number of empirical investigations which he claims reveal a clear sequence of stages in moral thinking. As people grow and interact with the environment, they go through these stages of moral thinking, starting from Stage 1, the lowest, and progressing on to successively higher stages. Each stage represents a structure of thinking, but Kohlberg's theory emphasizes the process, rather than the relative morality or immorality, of decisions involving moral issues.

Using hypothetical moral situations, Kohlberg and his colleagues have interviewed adults and children in the United States, in Britain, in Turkey, in Taiwan, and in Mexico about right and wrong. In these investigations he has found the same forms of moral thinking. Therefore, he has posited a six-stage sequence that he believes to be universal across all cultures. These stages are summarized in the table below.[2]

Levels	Basis of Moral Judgment	Stages of Development
I	Moral value resides in external, quasi-physical happenings, in bad acts, or in quasi-physical needs rather than in persons and standards.	*Stage 1:* Obedience and punishment orientation. Egocentric deference to superior power or prestige, or a trouble-avoiding set. Objective responsibility.
		Stage 2: Naively egoistic orientation. Right action is that instrumentally satisfying the self's needs and occasionally others'. Awareness of relativism of value to each actor's needs and perspective. Naive egalitarianism and ori-

entation to exchange and reciprocity.

II	Moral value resides in performing good or right roles, in maintaining the conventional order and the expectancies of others.	*Stage 3:* Good-boy orientation. Orientation to approval and to pleasing and helping others. Conformity to stereotypical images of majority or natural role behavior, and judgment by intentions.
III	Moral value resides in conformity by the self to shared or shareable standards, rights, or duties.	*Stage 4:* Authority and social-order maintaining orientation. Orientation to "doing duty" and to showing respect for authority and maintaining the given social order for its own sake. Regard for earned expectations of others.

Stage 5: Contractual legalistic orientation. Recognition of an arbitrary element or starting point in rules or expectations for the sake of agreement. Duty defined in terms of contract, general avoidance of violation of the will or rights of others, and majority will and welfare.

Stage 6: Conscience or principle orientation. Orientation not only to actually ordained social rules but to principles of choice involving appeal to logical universality and consistency. Orientation to conscience as a directing agent and to mutual respect and trust.

Each of these six general stages of moral orientation can be defined in terms of its specific stance on some 32 aspects of morality. For example, with regard to the aspect of "motivation for rule obedience or moral action," the six stages are defined as follows:[3]

Stage 1. Obey rules to avoid punishment.

Stage 2. Conform to obtain rewards, have favors returned, and so on.

Stage 3. Conform to avoid disapproval, dislike by others.

Stage 4. Conform to avoid censure by legitimate authorities and resultant guilt.

Stage 5. Conform to maintain the respect of the impartial spectator judging in terms of community welfare.

Stage 6. Conform to avoid self-condemnation.

It is evident that the six stages of this aspect of moral development represent successive degrees of internalization of moral sanctions. Other aspects of moral development involve successive cognitive reorganization of the meaning of culturally universal values. As an example, human life is a basic value in every society. However, each culture has its own definition of this value and its own conditions under which life may be sacrificed for some other value. With regard to the value of life, the six stages are defined as follows:[4]

Stage 1. The value of a human life is confused with the value of physical objects and is based on the social status of physical attributes of its possessor.

Stage 2. The value of a human life is seen as instrumental to the satisfaction of the needs of its possessor or of other persons.

Stage 3. The value of a human life is based on the empathy and affection of family members and others toward its possessor.

Stage 4. Life is conceived as sacred in terms of its place in a categorical moral or religious order of rights and duties.

Stage 5. Life is valued both in its relation to community welfare and as a universal human right.

Stage 6. Life is valued as sacred and as representing a

universal human value of respect for the individual.

Kohlberg's theory is a very positive one. His research suggests that certain kinds of intervention can help people advance through these stages. His work in schools shows that having children freely discuss moral dilemmas over a period of three or four months can help them gain one full stage. Kohlberg believes that his emphasis on the process of thought, rather than on specific moral outcomes, is a most appropriate stance for the public schools in a pluralistic society. Further, he claims that the U. S. Constitution is a "Stage 5 document," and that it is, therefore, a legitimate role of the schools to aid people to get to the stage where they fully understand and appreciate the Constitution. (Kohlberg has recently stated that the reason for Nixon's demise is that, not being a Stage 5 person, he really did not understand the Constitution. Kohlberg asserts that Nixon's public statements reveal him to be a Stage 4 Law and Order Authoritarian, while the presidential tapes reveal him to be a Stage 2 Naive Instrumental Hedonist.)

The Cognitive-Developmental Theory suggests that people make transition from one stage to the other as a result of cognitive conflict. Grappling with moral dilemmas and listening to the arguments at higher stages than one's own are key ingredients to moving up. However, current research indicates that people can only "take in" or fully understand moral reasoning at one level above their own. Moral thinking two levels or more above simply seems to wash over them, and, according to Kohlberg's theory, has no effect on moral development.

The Impact of Television on Morality

What possible connection does this new theory have with popular television? Although at this point I can only speculate, the following issues need to be considered. First, the great bulk of TV entertainment is composed of human beings struggling with moral problems. Second, these entertainments attempt to involve the viewer in moral problems, since the key characters in these dramas must choose between moral options: How should Archie Bunker respond to the arrival of a Black family in his immediate neighborhood? Should Mary Tyler Moore go out with this new man in her life now that she has discovered that he is married? Should Mannix deny the civil rights of someone who he is convinced is a murderer? Should Marcus Welby cooperate with a terminal cancer patient and let him take his own life? Should Pa Ingles move his family away from their home in Walnut Grove after a tornado has wiped out his crop? Much of the viewer's interest is generated by watching the main characters weighing costs and benefits of these alternatives. These ingredients are similar to those in the moral dilemmas which research by Kohlberg indicates are instrumental in moral stage movement.

On the other hand, the Cognitive-Developmental Approach to Moral Education may have less significance for television analysis because of some other factors. To begin with, television drama seems to have an "out there" quality for the viewer. How seriously does the young viewer get involved in Maude's moral struggles? Is he really touched by them and, if so, how deeply? In the same article referred to above, television critic Arlen suggests that we remember very little of these popular entertainments. If they do, in essence, go in one ear and out the other, what sort of "stage transition" effect could they have? Lastly, there are technical questions of whether or not television's moral messages fit the needs of the majority of its audience. Could the moral content of television shows be pitched at a level too high for most viewers, particularly the younger, lower-stage viewers, to absorb?

An initial slice into the problem. In order to see if Kohlberg's theory were at all useful in determining the moral impact of television drama, I decided to pick one television program and see how it related to some of the issues of moral development raised by the Cognitive-Developmental Theory. For pure personal convenience I chose an episode of "Kung Fu" entitled *The Predators*, which was shown May 10, 1975. Although I had never seen this show, I had a vague idea of its content from flicking through the channels and seeing a few spot ads. My impression was that it was about an oriental wanderer making his way through our wild west. The main character came through as an Eastern Johnny Appleseed, sowing the badlands with virtue and good works.

When I sat down to look at the show, I had three questions in mind. First, are the dilemmas presented moral in nature and how prominent are these dilemmas? Second, is each character in the episode clearly at a particular stage of moral thinking? And third, how does this TV program act as a moral educator, teaching about the rightness and wrongness of behavior, and can Kohlberg's Cognitive-Developmental Theory help answer this question?

Moral Dilemmas. This particular episode is full of moral dilemmas. It opens with some men asking the main character, Caine (who turns out to be half Chinese and half American), if he has seen an Apache. These men are obviously out to kill the Indian, and Caine, who has the Apache in view, is confronted with the dilemma of telling the truth (thereby becoming a probable cause of the Apache's murder) or telling a lie in order to shield the Apache. He answers by denying the meaning of the question and answering in a very strict way:

> Mountain Man: The brother of the one we shot. Where is he? We ain't going to ask you again . . .
>
> Caine: I see no Apache.

Shortly after this, Caine is caught up in what appears to be a continual tension between his role as Teacher of the Good Way and the safety of himself and of those around him.

The other characters, however, have more tangible dilemmas. The Apache is torn between his pledge to Caine (who saved his life) and the apparent tribal demand to kill Rafe, the Indian hunter who slew and scalped his brother. Much of the drama is involved with this struggle of conscience. It is finally resolved when the Apache rejects the opportunity to kill Rafe, and lives up to his pledge to Caine, although with some unhappiness.

Rafe, too, has his dilemmas. While most of them involve his own personal safety, he is continually being pressed by Caine to take on moral perspective. Caine tries to get him to live by his word, by his conscience. He is also trying to get him to live up to his obligation to be part of the legal system and testify in Caine's own defense in a murder trial.

As a characteristic of "Kung Fu," there is a parallel subplot consisting of flashbacks to an earlier time when Caine was a teenage Taoist monk in China. In this subplot, Teh Soong, a slightly older monk who is an in-training friend of Caine's, struggles with himself and with Caine over how best to serve humanity. Teh Soong apparently is consumed by a desire to see justice come to his people, and, therefore, decides to fight injustice directly by becoming a revolutionary. After several abortive attempts, he realizes that:

"... my cause was false. My concern only visited greater suffering upon the people. I sought my own glory."

He resolves his dilemma by returning to the monastery and following the ways of the Master.

There is one final dilemma that runs through the entire episode, including both the basic western plot and the eastern subplot. It is presented in the form of a question:

Caine: Master, wherein does brotherhood lie?

Caine's teacher endorses this as an important question:

Master: That is a question well worth asking (and sagely looking off into the distance)—well worth considering.

In the Chinese subplot, this particular question weaves its way through Caine's concern. What is his obligation to his friend Teh Soong? What is the Master's? This quest to find the meaning of brotherhood, of course, is the essence of Teh Soong's struggle to understand how to serve people.

In the occidental plot, Caine tries to show both Rafe and the Apache that they are joined by a common humanity. He is asking them to rise above their narrow tribal prejudices and acknowledge the universal principle of brotherhood. However, the Apache's desire for revenge, fully supported by his tribe, blocks his realization, while Rafe is limited by his own selfish desire for reward and a rather obvious, racially based contempt for Indians and half-breeds. Whether or not these dilemmas truly engage young viewers, and whether or not they cause any of the needed cognitive moral conflict, is, at this point, a matter for pure speculation. However, there can be little doubt that this particular program did present moral dilemmas to the viewer.

Moral State of Characters. Classifying an individual at a particular stage of moral development is not a casual activity. Kohlberg, in his interviews, would have an individual respond to three different dilemmas and then he would analyze the individual's responses for evidence of various kinds of stage reasoning. Typically, fifty percent of a person's responses fall into one stage and that person is, therefore, classified at that stage. Of course, Kohlberg's method of analysis is impossible in this exercise. However, the fictitious characters of this episode of "Kung Fu" were created to represent certain types, morally and otherwise, and their words and actions are available to our analysis. We can, therefore, make some primitive judgments about their stages of moral reasoning.

Rafe, the Indian hunter, would appear to be a Stage 2 Instrumental Hedonist. He hunts and scalps Indians for the satisfaction and financial reward it brings him. Except possibly at the very end of the drama, his concern is always for himself.

The Apache seems to be at Stage 4, one of the best of the Conventional Moral Thinkers. As a leader, he is concerned with the tribal code and he responds to arguments of honor and keeping one's word.

Then there is Teh Soong who appears to be at Stage 5. He is greatly concerned with justice and individual rights. However, he has not reached the point of recognizing the implications of the universal principles of brotherhood. Not inconsistent with Kohlberg's theory, Teh Soong's Stage 5 reasoning apparently was also infected with Stage 2 Instrumental Hedonism, in that he was searching for personal glory.

The Master and Caine are clearly Stage 6 moral reasoners. They continually exhibit principled, moral thinking. Although, in the earlier, Chinese subplot, Caine appears to be a Stage 5 student of his Stage 6 teacher, in the major plot, he has clearly arrived. He, like his Master, is continually attempting to live by the highest principles and help others to learn these principles.

In this episode, the major characters' stages of moral development were clearly discernible. Furthermore, one would guess that, in a television series (unlike a film), the viewer builds up a history of the characters and becomes familiar with the way they respond to moral questions.

"Kung Fu" as a Moral Educator. This episode dealt with universal brotherhood, racial tolerance, nonviolent behavior, the need for human trust, the dangers of giving in to revenge and other forms of anger, the idea that retribution comes to bullies, the folly of revolutionary activity, the concept of filial respect for elders, and the view that the meek, while not exactly inheriting the earth, can walk it unscathed. The clear benefits of taking on virtue and avoiding vice were borne out before our eyes. The completely good guys (Caine and Master) have transcended their enemies. The not-quite-so-good guys (the Apache and Teh Soong) run amuck, but then regain their footing on the true path. The one good-guy-gone-sour (the Indian

tracker) gets killed when he rejects good and engages in an act of violence. The major bad guy (Rafe) has a rebirth. And the rest of the bad guys (Rafe's gang) commit a gross act of cowardice by "high-tailing it," thus revealing their true colors.

This episode strongly suggests that Caine is playing a traditional role of a moral educator. Further, the outcomes of the plot reinforce widely held behavioral standards with the good being rewarded and the evil either being redeemed or punished. It is this simplistic quality that undoubtedly makes the Michael Arlens wince. On the other hand, there is an exposure to several different moral positions and justifications for actions that takes "Kung Fu" beyond the standard good guys versus bad guys conflict. Characters think out and live out their view of how and why one should behave. This, particularly from a Kohlbergian framework, gives "Kung Fu" a special dimension as a force for moral education.

Some Larger Issues. Viewing this episode of "Kung Fu" raises some other larger questions. What, if anything, did the viewer learn that might affect his behavior? Has this hour-long encounter with Caine deepened his understanding of what a good man is and how he should behave? Does the viewer get truly involved with Caine's plight so that he thinks along with Caine and the other characters, weighs moral alternatives, and otherwise receives a vicarious moral experience? Does he develop a positive feeling toward pacifism and an emotional distaste for violence?

Or, is the viewer just following the surface action, not really getting intellectually or emotionally involved enough to have his sense of morality challenged? While I suspect that this latter is the case for the majority of viewers the majority of the time, this does not negate the possibility of a significant impact on our thinking that results from watching a show like "Kung Fu" over an extended period of time. Nor does it negate the possibility of one episode having a strong influence on an individual's thinking. Does Caine and his way of thinking become familiar ground to the regular viewer? Does Caine's method of dealing with moral situations become an alternative for the viewer, one which he comes to understand and to which he is attracted?

Since most of us watch so much television and because it is so much a part of the lives of our children, it is difficult to imagine that television is not having a significant impact on our moral thinking and stage transitions as described by Kohlberg. While it may be high heresy to suggest that TV is having anything but a mind-rotting and morals-corrupting effect, it might possibly be that many types of TV adventures have a positive moral impact on their viewer.

Another essential question must be raised: How typical is "Kung Fu" of TV adventures? Since having viewed an episode of "Kung Fu," I have seen a public relations release by Warner Brothers, the producers of this series. Clearly, Warner Brothers sees the series as having a high moral impact, and, therefore, being a cut above the competition:

> Being with Caine in this television series affords us [Warner Brothers] a rare opportunity. . . .These incidents and dialogue, when reflected upon by viewers in Caine's life can doubtlessly effect positive emotional and psychic extensions. . . .Caine's deeply philosophical and stoic nature presents his immediate goals quite simply—harmony with man and nature; the basic essential human survival.

While "Kung Fu" appeared to cover a great deal of explicitly moral material, and presented it in an especially talkative fashion, it still employed those twin magnets of TV adventure: violence and mayhem. I suspect a good portion of "Kung Fu's" audience tuned in each week to see how Caine, master of the martial arts, did against the fast-draw, pistol-whipping, eye-gouging, bullyboys of the Old West. For this segment of the audience, the heavy beat of the physical action drum may have all but drowned out the fine and gentler contribution of the morally attuned string section. Nevertheless, there are those who attend particularly to the strings and hardly notice the percussion section. Yet, one wonders whether the reason that the "Kung Fu" series was cancelled (at the end of the 1975 season) was because there was too much moralizing and not enough mayhem. It might very well be that the writers were not skillful enough to bring together these two elements, to turn out weekly dramatic presentations with that combination of percussion and strings, violent action and engagement of our moral sensitivities, that marks dramas like *Othello* or even works closer in type to "Kung Fu" like "The Oxbow Incident."

How typical of TV heroes is Caine? While it is impossible to answer this question, it may be helpful to compare Caine with Messrs. Baretta and Kojak, the heroes of two newer and apparently more successful (larger audiences) adventure programs. For one thing, Caine is clearly a solid Stage 6, which is not the case with Baretta and Kojak. Each week amid the lollipops, parrots, and flashy street talk, we see Baretta and Kojak confronted with what are essentially moral dilemmas. And, each week before our eyes, we see these two television heroes work out their dilemmas in a fashion that is usually high-minded. While they are pulled by conflicting forces, they normally appear to rise above the conventional level (Stages 3 and 4) of moral thinking to Kohlberg's post-conventional levels (Stages 5 and 6). It is not so much, then, that Kojak and Baretta are fundamentally different from Caine. Rather, they are still on their way to the higher stages, while the saintly Caine has already arrived.

On the other hand, Kojak and Baretta, as teachers of the moral life, do have some qualities which clearly differentiate them from Caine. These factors, while addressing the moral dimensions of the programs, may also explain why they have been more popular than "Kung Fu." First, where Caine is a passive traveler-through-life, Kojak and Baretta are action-lawmen. They often take the law into their own hands, even though they are themselves lawmen. They are pale imitations of Dirty Harry, the avenging cop (from the movie of the same name), who goes outside the law in the service of justice. To this breed of lawman, civil rights and other individual liberties are legal niceties that are either ignored or finessed. While not as extreme as Dirty Harry, Baretta and Kojak often resort to threats, trickery and the strong arm. Caine gets involved in violent actions, but always against his will, always after he has tried to avoid it. He is never moved to anger. While Baretta and Kojak's rough stuff and flashes of anger give us visual excitement and make them more "entertaining," these very elements weaken their value as positive moral educators and soil them as moral models.

The shows differ on another dimension relating to their impact on public morality. "Kung Fu" is a period piece. Set in the Old West, it most likely carries with it for the viewer, the romantic, mythical trappings of the Western genre. The viewer probably settles in for those good old times when "men were men and women were wo- men." In contrast, the viewer watching Kojak or Baretta feels he is tuning in to a glimpse of the "real world," albeit a part of the world he doesn't actually have to bump into every day. Kojak and Baretta are *now*. They live and tell it like it is. If "Kung Fu" is perceived as romance, while Kojak and Baretta are perceived as realism, this probably effects the weight given by the viewer to whatever moral message resides in the shows. One might hazard the guess that the viewer takes his cues on how to behave from television's modern man rather than from its Western mystique. What these latter points are suggesting, then, is that the more typical and popular dramatic heroes present the viewer with a more ambiguous and occasionally dubious set of moral behaviors than does "Kung Fu's" Caine. While there is surely moral content and impact to the shows, the possible effects are not as clear.

We might also speculate that another reason "Kung Fu," in spite of the martial arts with flashing feet and chopping hands, never gained a big audience is that the moral dimension of the dramas was presented in an atypical manner. It might simply be that a relatively small percentage of the audience "decodes" Caine's and the Master's moral reasonings. If they are continually speaking to us at Stage 6 and the great bulk of us are only at Stage 3 and 4, then their words may be just washing over us. Other TV figures in the moral crunch, such as Baretta and Kojak, usually end up reasoning at Stage 5 (where they are still accessible to many viewers). But they often start out reasoning at a lower level and perhaps they are more likely to take the viewer with them. Besides the fact that Stage 6 reasoning has little meaning for most of us lesser men, there is also the suspicion that a great density of Stage 6 talk is simply not very dramatic for a mass audience.

Can Kohlberg Contribute to our Understanding of Television?

These "Kung Fu" issues aside, does Lawrence Kohlberg's Cognitive-Developmental Approach to Moral Education illuminate our understanding of television's impact on public morality? Is it a useful tool?

First, we must be clear that Lawrence Kohlberg's Cognitive-Developmental Theory of Moral Development is just that—a theory. It is still disputed whether or not this theory represents anything real in the world: whether there really are stages of moral development and whether we go through them as Kohlberg states. A recent issue of the *Psychological Bulletin* calls into question much of Kohlberg's research, primarily on methodological grounds.[5] And, if Kohlberg's measuring rod is in question, then so is the theory. Behaviorists and psychologists of other schools find Kohlberg's explanations much too speculative, much too intuitive. Philosophers, like Michael Scriven and R. S. Peters, find Kohlberg's theory helpful, but hardly the all-encompassing explanation that many of its advocates are suggesting.[6] To these philosophers, the Cognitive-Developmental Approach is simply one way to understand what is for them a much more complex phenomenon.

Conclusion

Even with these reservations in mind, Kohlberg's theory can still have real value for our understanding of the impact of TV on the moral development of the young. First, it gives us a new means to research the effect of television on the moral thinking of young viewers. A cognitive-developmental test of stages can be an important measuring tool to see if, and to what degree, dramas influence the moral thinking of the young. The short term and, particularly, the long term effects of TV drama viewing on moral thinking, and possibly even on moral behavior, cannot be investigated. Further, we might be able, through careful experimentation, to discern the effects of the same TV moral message on viewers who are at different stages of development.

A more immediate and practical use of this theory could be simply to help us understand more thoroughly what is going on in TV dramas. It would help us understand that much of the conflict in these adventures is not just a clash of value systems, but different levels of moral thinking coming in conflict.

Kohlberg's stage theory of moral development can be useful to parents and educators because it provides them with a language and a system to focus on ethical and moral issues which are raised by television adventures. It enables them first to decode the thinking of different characters as they deal with moral issues. Along with this understanding and having some appreciation of the stages of the viewers, the adult is ready to engage the young in a discussion of the moral meaning of what they have seen on television.

The great promise of Kohlberg's theory, then, is that it can help us move beyond the rhetoric that surrounds discussions of television's impact on public morals and begin to analyze the influence of this great force on our ways of thinking about right and wrong.

Footnotes

1. Kevin Ryan and Michael G. Thompson. "Moral Education's Muddled Mandate: Comments on a Survey of Phi Delta Kappans," *Phi Delta Kappan*, June 1975 (Volume LVI, No. 10, pp. 663-666).

2. L. Kohlberg. "Education for Justice, A Modern Statement of the Platonic View," in Sizer, ed., *Moral Education* (Harvard University Press, 1970).

3. L. Kohlberg. "Moral Development," *International Encyclopedia of the Social Sciences* (Crowell, Collier and MacMillan, Inc., 1968), pp. 489-494.

4. Op. cit.

5. William Kurtines and Esther B. Grief. "The Development of Moral Thought: Review and Evaluation of Kohlberg's Approach," *Psychological Bulletin*, August, 1974 (Volume LXXXI, No. 8, pp. 453-470).

6. Michael Scriven. "Cognitive Moral Development," *Phi Delta Kappan*, June, 1975 (Volume LVI, No. 10, pp. 689-694). Richard S. Peters. "A Reply to Kohlberg," *Phi Delta Kappan*, June, 1975 (Volume LVI, No. 10, pp. 678).

Television News
as Narrative

Sharon Lynn Sperry

Network television is the primary source of news for more than half of the American public.[1] Moreover, the newsman, particularly the anchorman, is an object of special affection from that public. Walter Cronkite, for instance, has enjoyed a higher popularity rating than most contenders for public office and some incumbent Presidents. Television news itself continues to attract an increasingly loyal and trusting audience. Roper Research Associates' periodic studies of the various news media reveal that 51 percent of the respondents in 1974 thought television was the most believable of the news media. That figure represented a significant jump from 1959, when only 29 percent of the Roper sample stated their faith in TV news.[2] The 1974 survey also demonstrated, for the first time in the 15 years of the Roper poll, that a majority of college-educated respondents (56 percent) preferred television as their main source of news.

It is noteworthy that the believability of the TV news medium has grown in the very years when American institutions generally,

Ms. Sperry is a doctoral candidate in English at Indiana University and teacher of a course on television there. She is also coordinator of a television project and administrative assistant at The Poynter Center.

and government particularly, have suffered from a much-cited credibility gap.[3] What is even more interesting is that journalism as a profession has come under serious and sustained attack during these years—and not merely from politicians and citizens' lobbies with self-serving motives. For every *public* voice attacking the credibility of journalists, we also hear, or at least sense, an uneasy choral response rippling through the country.

Certainly, TV newsmen feel that critics are lurking in every living room. Walter Cronkite cannot have been speaking only to the likes of Clay Whitehead or Spiro Agnew when, on returning from a Christmas vacation on January 6, 1975—a time when neither Whitehead nor Agnew was around to nettle him—he felt compelled to address these unseen critics:

> Good evening. Well, one can sail away through the islands of the Caribbean out of touch with daily newspapers, radio, and television and one can begin to believe as all the good news advocates keep pointing out to us that the world isn't in nearly as bad a shape as it appears through the news dispatches that cross this desk each night. And then you come back to the rude awakening. The news makers just won't cooperate. As long as they're making the decisions that affect our lives in this complex society, we'd better know what they're up to, unpleasant or not. We can bury our heads in the sand at our peril. There aren't many smart ostriches. So here goes today's report.

The situation resists easy explanation. Newsmen are under general attack, but television newsmen are nevertheless watched and believed by the greatest percentage of the population. Numerous articles and books take television to task for sensationalizing the news, for hyping conflict, for over-simplifying events, and skimming the surface. More bitter critics accuse the national news media, television included, of ideological bias. Television, particularly, is blamed for public apathy and voter cynicism.[4]

Some of those accusations can be answered satisfactorily. Some are valid and ought to lead to changed performance. But none have dealt adequately with the question of why television journalism, as we know it in the network evening news, has been able to build a large and loving audience in a decade when journalism generally is a suspect institution in the public mind.

It is my opinion that the explanation resides, not in the literal content of television news, but in the implicit content of its architecture. By examining the structure, the subtle internal form of the half-hour network news program, we really begin to see what it is that makes television news the most popular—and controversial—brand of journalism.

This examination must begin by recognizing that the national television news shows stand at the front of prime-time programming each evening, and that the networks expect the news to capture an early audience which will stay tuned for the rest of the evening's programs. Consequently, the networks pour their resources into the half-hour news shows with an eye to building an audience as well as to fulfilling their responsibilities for news coverage. This policy, in turn, sets the parameters for the form that the news assumes: half an hour's worth of news *stories*. Television news is a blend of traditional, objective journalism and a kind of quasi-fictional prime-time story-telling which frames events in reduced terms with simple, clear-cut values.

In other words, if the target audience for network news is that group of people who will tune in to "Kojak," or "Columbo," or "Baretta," it is natural to offer them news in a form congruent with their expectations for those later programs. Bound to report the day's events accurately, and prevented from creating convenient and attractive fictions, the network executives' only recourse is to adopt the same structure which the entertainment programs assume —namely, the telling of a story. Understanding this, we might usefully apply narrative theory to television in general, and television news in particular, in order to reveal the peculiar structure of television news and the reasons that these programs so attract their audiences.

Narrative Theory

Narrative theory, as it has been developed by literary critics, is the examination of the strategic and aesthetic devices which develop when someone tells a story to a reader or a listener. Narrative is a form as ancient as human speech. Man is a shape-maker, a metaphorist, an incorrigible imagist. To know and give order to the world he lives in, man has always devised and shared stories.

There are three elements in the narrative mixture: teller, tale, and listener. The two human elements act in concert to relay the tale, which can be fact or fiction, philosophical speculation or scientific definition or metaphorical explanation. When the narrative presumes to present fact—Truth—it is understood that that Truth is necessarily approximate; for it must be filtered through the point of view of the narrator. Like the fictional narrative, the nonfiction narrative must also be pruned and shaped by the narrator if it is to accomplish its goal; for that goal is not merely to provide information but also to affect the listener in some way: to persuade or change him, to evoke an emotional response, or simply to interest him.

The nonfiction narrative form demands these compromises of the Truth—a point of view and a shaping and simplification. And, by both tradition and necessity, the listener assents to these narrative necessities. There is a "willing suspension of disbelief" by the listener, and an agreement by the narrator to approximate reality as he has seen or heard it. This agreement by the two is based on an understanding that the narrator has struck the right compromise between Truth (the chaos of reality) and the listener's expectation of a coherent and effective (or affective) form.

The credibility of the narrator is the key to this understanding, and for this the teller must possess authority. Seeking authority—credibility—for the point of view is an indigenous narrative problem —a challenge to narrators as old as Homer and as recent as Walter Cronkite. It is this struggle for authority which marks the TV newsman most conspicuously as a member of the narrative clan.

The Anchorman as Narrator

In every narrative, the narrator—the authority who tells the story—is of primary importance, and this must be true for the television news program as for any other narrative. Consequently, the structural pattern for the half-hour program is directly tied to the function of the anchorman. He is the one who stands in the position of the author of the tale: the ultimate narrator.

Each news story, although relayed by individual correspondents, is framed by the presence of the anchorman. It is the anchorman who reads all the briefer reports and who introduces each filmed report with a line or two, indicating that he commands the substance of all the reports.

ABC NEWS. Tuesday, December 3, 1974. Harry Reasoner in New York introduces the first story with these words:

Representative Wilbur Mills, until recently perhaps the most powerful man in Congress, has been admitted to Bethesda Naval Hospital just outside Washington. A hospital spokesman said Mills entered the hospital in midafternoon but gave no other details. For some time Mills has reportedly suffered from ill health. Last year he was away from his office for an extended period with a back ailment. More recently the Congressman has had serious problems as a result of his association with a striptease dancer. Some of Mills' power in the House Ways and Means Committee has already been taken away by the Democratic Caucus in the House. Earlier, before Mills entered the hospital today, some of his close associates were even saying he might resign from Congress. ABC Capitol Hill correspondent Bob Clark has more.

That "more" will be the first story of the night, and though it may sometimes include a film, it will always have a narrative. By introducing these stories as he does, the anchorman implies that he has control over them. In reality, he may never have seen the film before, but his words still suggest absolute control. The anchorman is, in effect, a corporate creature, the human representative of the central monolith which is the single television screen. Whatever developing theme the half-hour assumes is pinned to his constant presence in the interspaces of the program. His words move the program along, linking story to story according to some larger pattern of meaning, as if the stories of the half-hour were thoughts from his single mind, ordered and moving in rational progression.

The anchorman is omnipresent and, standing in the center of the events he presents, his tone is omnipotent. Even when he disdains omnipotence and expresses tentative doubts, as John Chancellor sometimes does, he cannot escape the fact that he sits in New York, at the command desk, and marshals the evening's program. His audience necessarily perceives him as holding a position of superior knowledge. His function is to provide the only available effective model for action and answers, because he alone commands the whole body of problems, conflicts, and characters, and he alone provides the continuous thread of meaning. It is in this function that he derives the trust and admiration of the audience. He has ritualized the presentation of the news, and in that ritual, lies the audience's only security. It is a curious security, as we shall see.

The Hero Plot in TV News

Prime-time television entertainment is made up mainly of plotted hero stories—simple, evocative, and, therefore, effective narratives. Each story assumes a line of action which is built around a few regular characters. A number of lesser characters, usually bearing the problem that sets the plot in motion, appear for a single episode and then disappear at the end of that episode when their problem has been resolved by the regulars. The plot is always one of overt action. Thought, emotional growth, and cognitive recognition have never been a priority on television except as they assume the explicit shape of action. A problem arises and the main character, the protagonist, with the support of the few regulars who make up the continuing cast, jails the crook, or saves the fatally ill woman, or finally speaks his mind to the obstreperous neighbor. Most of these programs, whether dramatic or comic, are hero stories designed, in Richard Carpenter's words, to "celebrate the conquest over evil within a highly ritualized contest."

Such a pattern, repeated night after night in dozens of versions all portraying the same basic theme, implies that the TV audience derives satisfaction from a ritual formalization of ingrained feelings that the evil in the world can be overcome by men working together under the guidance of a leader.[5]

The narrative plot of action for television programming taps the roots of man's simplest and most pervasive myth: Men muddle through life as best they can, but when tragedy strikes, they require and seek a leader, a single individual of superior worth and superior skill, who will meet the problem and conquer the evil. The story is told everywhere in every type of communicative form: *The Odyssey*, *Beowulf*, "Anthony and Cleopatra," "The Lone Ranger," "A Man for All Seasons," "Kojak."

As the keystone of each network's evening programming, television news attempts to build and hold its audience by lifting elements of that mythic formula which is the basis of its entertainment programs. Av Westin, former president of ABC News, says that he expects an audience to come to his news program asking "Is the world safe, and am I secure?"[6] There is clearly a link between that question and the answer provided by a news structure that plots events directly along the lines of the hero story:

The world at peace is disrupted by some event (say, an act of terrorism). That event, which becomes the evil, is named and, if possible, analyzed and understood. It is then attacked by some leader, the hero figure, often a representative of the people. However, this leader, whether by choice or by the nature of his vocation, may not be able to meet the problem alone. So he gains allies, other leaders, and he also gains enemies—potential leaders who disagree with his plan of action, or rebels who align themselves with the evil. As these alignments become apparent, stories are then told of the effect of the problem on the average man. And, if the alignments become a matter more significant than the original event, we will also hear about the suffering of the average man as his appointed leaders fail to meet the problem. Eventually, the disruption is settled or forgotten, and the world returns to its original state of rest and security.

There is a primary problem with this structure of the news as hero story. The world and the world on television news are never really at rest or in security. The answer to Westin's question is inevitably, "No, the world is not secure, nor, perhaps, am I." Problems on television news do not end; they are only replaced on the agenda by new problems—Vietnam becomes Angola; one terrorist act becomes many successive acts; Charles Manson becomes Squeaky Fromme, who has taken the mantle of Lee Harvey Oswald.

Despite this incongruity, television news remains tied to the structure of a hero plot: A conflict involving a small cast of characters arises from the introduction of a problem. The problem is to be solved by some representative protagonist whose activity on behalf of the people is designed to ensure that good will prevail.

We can choose any night at random, on any of the networks, and observe the formula unfolding:

> September 19, 1974. CBS EVENING NEWS. Roger Mudd sits in for Walter Cronkite.
>
> Special prosecutor Jaworski wants to summon former President Nixon to testify in the Watergate trial in order to substantiate the state's use of the White House tapes as evidence.
>
> The figure of Fred Graham appears, standing in front of the federal courthouse. Graham tells us that if Nixon pleads ill health, Judge Sirica will probably send a court-appointed doctor to examine him. The pre-trial hearing is scheduled for Tuesday.

The first stories of every newscast are generally the tales of mighty figures in public life, and one such cast can be with us for a long time.[7] Like soap operas, news stories often involve a set of major characters whose activities continue for months and even years. You may miss several passages of the story and still remain familiar with the major characters and their problems. Here, the characters—Nixon, the Watergate defendants, Judge Sirica, and Leon Jaworski—have become "regulars" appearing many times throughout several weeks of the news program, each time in the context of a new problem that derives from their special relationship with one another.

In this particular story, the roles and principles are clear. In simple terms, Jaworski is the protagonist, representing the law of the land, who is striving to conquer the evil of lawlessness. Judge Sirica is his supporting ally, who is about to send a new character, a doctor, to California to examine Nixon. That doctor, like a secondary character in "Petrocelli," will appear once, do his job, and disappear, setting the stage for the solution to the problem. The minor plot of getting the White House tapes verified as trial evidence is easily enough resolved in a few installments; but the larger context of the drama, involving how these characters will work against each other through the many complications implicit in their roles, will take many weeks, perhaps months.

The story has an extended interest because one of the major characters, Nixon, has shifted from his one-time role as a protagonist—as President—to an antagonist, at odds with the workings of the protagonist and associated with the villains of the story, the Watergate defendants.* None of this is deliberately ideological. Ideology has no relevance here at all. If you tell the news as a story, and if the story form you have chosen is a heroic tale, then there must be a protagonist and an antagonist. It is not political favoritism but simply a formulaic understanding of how the world operates.

Each individual news story, then, is a small but distinct narrative, with a recognizable plot of action which sets character against character in a struggle to redeem the world. A larger pattern becomes visible as story follows story in the half-hour news show. The conflicts are staked in greater issues, become more abstract in nature, and are less available to direct action on the part of any one character or group of characters. There is evil afoot, but it cannot be clearly identified, and the usual channels for discovering it are bogging down. Action and resolution become increasingly difficult, yet action is the only alternative when the structure of the stories pits character against character.

Another story on the same CBS News program illustrates the problem:

> HEW, Mudd reports, has convened a conference of business leaders to discuss the economy and a special committee of Congress is also investigating the state of the economy. To report on the congressional investigation, Daniel Schorr appears.
>
> Senator Kennedy, a member of the committee, urges them to focus on the forgotten. He attacks Greenspan, who has come to testify, for penalizing the poor. Greenspan replies on film.
>
> All of us are suffering, he says, but the Wall Street brokers are hit the hardest. Laughter follows. Someone shouts "face facts" and there are cries from the audience in the chamber.

---

*I would submit that one of the reasons television was slower than the other news media to investigate Watergate was that the President, by nature, is a protagonist. Only when overwhelming evidence began to shift the weight of positive action to others—the courts, primarily—did Nixon's image as protagonist begin to diminish on television. Such a shift of characterization is nearly impossible in the dramatic format of nightly television, where the lines of force for good and evil are sharply rigid, and a story cleanly begins and ends with the roles of hero and villain intact.

In this story, the simple hero plot, in which evil and good are clear and the line of action is obvious, begins to turn on itself. The evil in this second story is an ambiguous force, the erratic economy, which is not an evil which can be readily analyzed or understood. It can be known only by its symptoms (the price of groceries, the loss of jobs, etc.), and even these symptoms do not lend themselves easily to the demands of film for action. Our constituted leader, the available protagonist, is a Senator. Yet the plot of the story limits this new protagonist's ability. The economic problem is a disembodied miasma. Kennedy can lead an investigation, but unlike Jaworski or Sirica, he cannot eventually resolve the problem, even after a whole series of news stories concerned with this "plot."

When complaints, investigations, and issued statements are the only actions, and when faces are continually present and continually talking at us or at each other but rarely acting, we know we are in the presence of an ineffective protagonist and failed narrative. Before our eyes, Kennedy has scored a point against Greenspan and is applauded by the audience in the chamber. But by structuring the story of the economic disruption in this way, the television newsmen have conveyed a faulty message. Implicit in their coverage, and in the customary expectations of the audience is the notion that Kennedy's simple act can settle the problem. The economic difficulties of the nation and the philosophical conflict between the two political parties are symbolized (and simplified) by this one-on-one televised confrontation. Yet, the contrary tones of ultimate failure and impotence in dealing with the real problem create an oxymoron: the semblance of action which has no force of action in it. Kennedy's —the protagonist's—action does not change the situation, does not redeem the actor or his community.

The Need for Action and News Perspectives in TV News

Both the Watergate story and the Kennedy committee hearings on the economy illustrate two other problems peculiar to news coverage on television. Filmed hearings or statements or news analyses are not the stuff of drama. The medium—the broadcast motion picture—requires movement, action, if it is to hold the attention and interest of its viewers. Thus, television news is frequently compelled to create action where none exists by "confronting" opposing leaders in a series of quick-cut statements, by developing a hero plot with the depiction of the "average man's" activities in coping with an intangible but newsworthy issue, and, most controversially, by selecting and focusing on a lesser but dramatizable moment from within a larger, more significant, but wholly undramatic context.

The other problem of TV news is freshness. In dealing with news stories which recur night after night, week after week—the Vietnam War, the Middle East crisis, the Watergate scandal—the network newsmen must contend with the probability of audience boredom. How often in the 1960s did we see a network correspondent, hunkered down in a steamy landscape, saying: "The bombs are falling on us here"? How inured did we all become to the bloodshed and tragedy shown nightly on our TV screens?

TV news programs seek viewer interest and loyalty, and they also accept a responsibility to *involve* the viewer, to help the American public understand and feel the issue at hand. Thus, the networks necessarily attempt to offer new perspectives and fresh insights in covering "old" but continuing news stories. One narrative device that they have adopted to solve this problem is the microcosmic and metaphoric feature story:

Saturday, May 3, 1975. CBS EVENING NEWS. The last Americans left Vietnam 24 hours earlier. Morton Dean reports that a young Vietnam veteran who was once a hawk has begun to speak softly of the "wasted" deaths of his friends in a war that no longer has meaning for him. His own voice from the past chants a pro-war song as the film cuts to the contemporary scene: the subdued mumble in a Louisiana bar and his own bearded face.

It is not useful to discuss such a news story—and there are many like it—in terms of fact or fiction, truth or falsehood. Credibility here is not so much a matter of empiricism as of an understanding by the audience that the newscaster has struck the right compromise. The audience assents to the narrative assumptions. What are those assumptions? For one, we know that what Morton Dean has reported is both true and false. We know that America is dissatisfied, even angry with the Vietnamese adventure and depressed by its meaninglessness. We know that there are many other young men like this veteran. We also know that the issues and the changes in attitude toward the war are not as simple as this young man's transition from singing a war ballad to growing a beard. We know that all events are not so easily structured along novelistic lines—protagonist blind, protagonist awakened—that not all young men who grow dissatisfied can articulate the issue so economically and effectively.

Morton Dean created a metaphor, and as with every metaphor, it is both a real report on our world, and a false, oversimplified presentation of a much more politically and emotionally complex issue. The agreement between viewer and narrator is to admit the need to simplify in order to say something which is approximately true. In this case, granting Morton Dean's and CBS News' credibility, the audience agrees willingly to the metaphorical act.

Not every news story strikes as successful a balance as Dean's did:

> Friday, November 8, 1974. CBS EVENING NEWS. David Dick reports from Tennessee that the Tom Marlow family have been barely surviving on a monthly welfare check ever since Tom Marlow was injured in a mining accident eleven years earlier. Against the backdrop of the World Food Conference, Walter Cronkite reminds us that there is hunger in America.

The next Monday a follow-up is necessary because calls poured into the CBS Studio over the weekend and envelopes stuffed with money arrived at the Marlows'. David Dick and Walter Cronkite explain patiently that it had not been the intention of CBS to make a special plea for one family; others were worse off than Tom Marlow. The point of their story was that Americans should not lose sight of poverty at home as we listen to talk of hunger abroad.

Something went wrong in the original story, or else a follow-up—a correction of an error—would not have been necessary. Again, there is no way to analyze the failure in terms of truth or falsehood. The journalistic response to the problem would, I suspect, be a comment about the viewers only hearing and seeing what they want to hear and see—not an untrue statement, by any means, but not a very useful one. Once it has been said, what is to be made of it? Isn't it, rather, a bit more helpful to realize that the assumption at the base of David Dick's narrative construct is an invitation to the audience to respond emotionally—a response which has its roots in storymaking, in the narrative function?

Dick created not a factual presentation (the stock market report is a factual presentation and, therefore, the least interesting segment of any news program), but a humanly motivated story. A news narrative, as does any narrative, engages the imaginative—hence, inevitably, emotional—response of the viewer. Narrative asks what are they like, why do they act, how does it feel, and invites the attendant emotional, imaginative realization of those questions. To expect the American viewer to sit in cold contemplation as a hungry American family is singled out is as impossible as if Dickens had forbidden weeping at the death of Little Nell. One compacts certain terms with any audience in the act of narration, and to expect to go around or under or over those terms, to expect to check their consequence, is to fail to understand the rules of the game. It is—to borrow from Scholes and Kellogg[8]—to expect to have your empirical bread and eat your narrative cake.

Cognition, in such a case, is distant. The reality of the narrative is the viewer's emotional reaction, and emotional engagement is the trickiest of relationships to predict or understand. Aristotle was hard put to explain it, and nobody after him has managed to clarify whether emotions are purged or incited by narrative presentation. What TV newsmen *do* know is that stories given to the depiction of elemental human dilemmas will galvanize emotion, and they will attract and maintain an audience.

A Challenge for New Forms in TV Newscasts

By structuring an event as a plotted story, involving all the drama of filmed confrontation (which is the preferred stock of television news) and the portrayal of complex matters in terms of simple conflict (which could be transferred without substantial change to an entertainment program), the television newsman deliberately invites his audience to respond to the news in the same way that it responds to entertainment programming. But news stories can never share the opening stasis and closing return to stasis of the heroic plot structure. The story (and the protagonist) is never able to achieve completion and never returns the world to a state of safe stability. We can vote the bums out of office, but each new set of leaders deals with nearly identical problems in the same ineffective ways. Not finding Jimmy Hoffa's body, or even a concrete crime connected with his disappearance, is the characteristic shape which events assume on television. The problem is carefully presented and detailed by filmed interviews. The leaders are seen working toward its solution. Then the story slowly fades away, usually unresolved. Hoffa's body hasn't turned up and no crime has been identified.

Not that the newsman should or could present a resolution where none exists. But in introducing action and simplifying conflict in order to dramatize the news and attract an audience, the television newsman can hardly escape the public frustration that surfaces when he fails to close his drama in some way more satisfactory than "That's the way it is."

The newsman, and the anchorman in particular, also disappoints the audience through his constant objectivity and dispassion. He should be a hero of action. He is the only character in the drama who commands the information, the resources, and the unsullied stature to act. He brings together the events of the world, summons the storytellers to relate their plots, and structures the whole into a recognizable and ritualized pattern. If the audience were able to accept the premise of his role—that knowing is the only action possible—he would succeed. But the various plots which constitute his knowledge and his story-telling are based on another premise: that knowing is related to the ability to act and that plotted action leads to resolution. As a result, the anchorman must forever assume a role fragmented by his inability to resolve problems or offer a concluding act. He is limited to telling the stories.

Changing the character of the anchorman—as John Chancellor has tried—will not alter the situation. We know from earlier experience at the BBC that no matter how conscientiously the newsman tries to act as a neutral announcer within a structure which casts him in a role as an authority, he will fail. British audiences were, for a time, witness to newsmen who tried to erase all suggestive implications in their delivery, but the vocal mannerisms which distinguish one human being from another inevitably emerged, and the audience quickly seized on favorites. Characterization is an element in narrative structure. Thus, as long as the TV news structure forces a person to sit as the functional authority, his character is manifested in that role.

One could say that television viewers ought to be capable of distinguishing between the clear-cut, repetitious resolutions of prime-time entertainment and the necessarily open-ended news stories of a world forever in transition, forever becoming. One could say that, if we didn't see the news programs, night after night, structuring the news events as narrative stories. Certainly, we can understand the networks' concern with building an audience for their news shows. And, perhaps, on a rational level, television audiences realize that the news is, by nature, fragmentary—a cyclical, unending series of events. In a sense, there is a kind of agreement between the networks and newsmen who present the news and the audience who views it: The newsmen recognize the need to structure the news so as to make it entertaining, while the audience recognizes that this entertaining narrative structure does not actually reflect the real world.

Yet, the narrative structure of the news programs still lead us to *emotionally* expect the congruence to be found in traditional narratives. That is, although we may understand why TV news is structured as it is, and why that structure does not always work out, we still somehow expect the narrative promise of wholeness and completion. And because this promise is not fulfilled—can never be fulfilled—we may feel disappointed and even antagonistic toward news shows and newsmen.

Network news has pandered for too long to the formula which fills most of the night's programming. Rather than counter the fragmentary nature of the news by superimposing forms on it which promise wholeness, television news should seek methods which will allow the fragmentation of news content to find its own complementary form. What those forms might be are perhaps suggested in programs like "Washington Week in Review" on PBS.

Whereas the core meanings of commercial network news lie in filmed narratives, and the structure of those narratives put the newsman, and the anchorman in particular, into the authoritative, authorial role, "Washington Week in Review" derives its energy from human conversation. The attention is shifted directly to the newsman, the story is known only from his discussion of it. The result is an attention to the human act of interpretation. Paradoxically, the newsman's role as an authority is made less significant when we see him develop his story, rather informally, before our eyes. Each reporter is also subject to question and disagreement from colleagues sitting around the table, and the moderator, Paul Duke, is cast more as a convener than as an anchorman.

The solution seems to be, then, not to remove the newsman from our attention, not to place him or her behind the story, but to make the newsman as newsman a part of the story. Only Charles Kuralt achieves that role on network news. The distinction between his human interest reports and hard news is less in the lighter content of his reportage than in the manner of it. Kuralt appears as part of his stories and, by doing so, enforces our awareness that he alone interpreted these events and in that aloneness is subject to judgment.

Footnotes

1. Roper Research Associates report for the Television Information Office, released at the National Association of Broadcasters, April 1975. *Broadcasting*, 88 (April 14, 1975), pp. 48-50.

2. "If you got conflicting or different reports of the same news story from radio, television, the magazines and the newspapers, which of the four versions would you be most inclined to believe—the one on radio or television or magazines or newspapers?"

	12/59	11/61	11/64	11/68	11/72	11/74
	%	%	%	%	%	%
TV	29	39	41	44	48	51
Newsp.	32	24	23	21	21	20
Radio	12	12	8	8	8	8
Mag.	10	10	10	11	10	8
DK/NA	17	17	18	16	13	13

3. "In April 1974, *U.S. News and World Report* asked five hundred U.S. 'leaders' to rate organizations and institutions according to the amount of influence . . . for decisions or actions affecting the nation as a whole. TV came in first, with a score of 7.2 on a scale of 1 to 10. The White House tied the Supreme Court for second place, and newspapers came next. In Burns Roper's 1973 report on the information preferences of the nation, TV was still at the top, with 64 percent of the population.

"In a special study done by Louis Harris for the Senate Subcommittee on Intergovernmental Relations, TV news was found to have made by far the greatest gains in public confidence since 1965—overtaking the military, organized religion, the Supreme Court, the U.S. Senate, the House of Representatives, and the executive branch of the federal government." — Marvin Barrett, ed., *Moments of Truth: The Fifth Alfred I. Dupont-Columbia University Survey of Broadcast Journalism*. New York: Thomas Y. Crowell Co., 1975, page 137.

4. See, for instance, Michael J. Robinson, "American Political Legitimacy in an Era of Electronic Journalism: Reflections on the Evening News," *Television as a Social Force: New Approaches to TV Criticism*, edited by Richard Adler. New York: Praeger Publishers, 1975.

5. Richard Carpenter, "Ritual, Aesthetics, and TV," *Journal of Popular Culture* (Fall, 1969); reprinted in *Mass Media and Mass Man*, edited by Alan Casty. New York: Holt, Rinehart and Winston, 1968.

6. Robert Daley, "We Deal With Emotional Facts," *New York Times Magazine* (December 15, 1974).

7. In an unpublished essay, Madonna Kolbenschlag of Notre Dame writes of the mirroring in television news of the hierarchy of story types established by Northrup Frye via Aristotle. First came the epics—superior characters in superior circumstances; then the hero tales—superior characters in ordinary circumstances; next, the melodramas—ordinary characters in ordinary circumstances; and finally, the low comedy—characters we can look down on who do not manage the everyday very well. Hughes Rudd is a genius at ending his morning news program on this last type.

8. Robert Scholes and Robert Kellogg, *The Nature of Narrative*. New York: Oxford University Press, 1966.

146

Thoughts on
Television Criticism

David Littlejohn

Television desperately needs criticism. Whether it gets the
kind of criticism it needs is something else again. The great
majority of the bashes aimed against it are superficial,
aimless, uninformed, distinguished by fury rather than
fact.

> —Hubbell Robinson, Jr.
> (former CBS Vice-President)
> "The Hatchet Men"
> *Saturday Review*
> (March 14, 1959)

. . . far too many TV critics in 1974 are continuing the
mindless—and anti-journalistic—practice of grinding out
fan-rot nonsense culled directly from network press
releases, or writing up fluffy and soporific phone interviews with fifth-billed stars of "Movie of the Week," or

Mr. Littlejohn is Professor and Acting Dean of the School of Journalism, University of California at Berkeley. He is the author or
editor of six books of literary criticism and biography. He has
written and broadcast critical reviews for public television, and has
served as a member of the TV Workshop Steering Committee.

spending hours in the unwarranted creation of "mailbox columns" filled with phony queries.

—Gary Deeb
(former television critic for
the *Chicago Tribune*)
"TV Critics—The Hack Pack"
Variety (January 9, 1974)

Television criticism in this country has been regarded with scorn almost from the start. Its practitioners have been called incompetent, superficial, and corrupt not only by media professionals (who might be expected to take offense), but by television critics themselves. In a 1959 survey commissioned by the Fund for the Republic, Patrick McGrady, Jr. wrote: "Television criticism is, by and large, the fitful labor of tired writers of monumental good will, a degree of talent and jaded perspective. As such, its effect is . . . generally inconsistent, capricious and of questionable value to anyone." He characterized Jack Gould, TV editor at *The New York Times* until 1971—and the most prolific, most powerful regular television writer this country has ever known—as "the poorest of the major critics . . . gratingly insensitive and illogical . . . objectionable, whimsical and, perhaps, dangerous." A fellow reviewer (Richard Burgheim of *Time*) once called Gould "a menace as a reporter," a man in need of "vocational guidance."

Have our television critics been as bad as these citations assert? Does any one among them, during the years between 1949 and 1974, stand out as distinctive and worth rereading—and if so, for what reasons? What qualities, forms, and standards are common to television criticism? Are there special problems or limitations built into the job which distinguish it from other forms of reviewing? Are there untried or under-used approaches to criticism which might be considered by the observers of American television's second quarter-century? These are some of the questions I would like to raise, and begin to answer.

Let me describe, first of all, how this project began and developed. It grew out of three presumptions:

(1) Television criticism in this country is, in general, of a very low order—considerably below the standards set

by the better American criticism of film, drama, art, music and literature. Moreover, this criticism is unworthy of the immense influence (and occasional high achievements) of the medium.

(2) There may be a number of ways to stimulate a television criticism that is better written, better informed, more penetrating, more responsive to both the nature of the medium and the surrounding social context, and, finally, more useful to both the industry and the viewers.

(3) Any discussion of future models for American television criticism will be more rational and realistic if it is based on a judicious summary of the work done in this field over TV's first 25 years.

I began by collecting references to all the reviews and articles concerning television that had appeared between 1949 and 1974 in 30 national general-interest magazines and in hundreds of other American and British periodicals of more specialized interest, as well as several masters' theses and doctoral dissertations. I read most of the critical pieces during this period from *Commentary*, *The Nation*, *The New Republic*, *The New Yorker*, *The New York Times Magazine*, and *The Reporter*, and a sampling from *The Atlantic Monthly*, *Newsweek*, *Saturday Review*, and *Time*—a total of about 800 reviews. I also discovered at least 200 *books* about television (including collected reviews by critics like Michael Arlen, John Crosby, Gilbert Seldes, and Robert Lewis Shayon) and read many of them. Finally, I reviewed essays and criticism of television by literary critics and cultural historians (Boorstin, Hentoff, Hoggart, Podhoretz, Trilling, Vidal), film and drama critics (Alpert, Hewes, Kael, Kanfer, MacDonald, Schickel, Tynan), and even music critics like Irving Kolodin and Winthrop Sargeant, who review televised operas and concerts.

Of course, the great bulk of television reviewing appears in daily newspapers across the country. This presents a formidable problem of access and research, but I was fortunate enough to acquire, as a start, the complete sets of newspaper columns and articles by two veteran practitioners, Jack Gould of *The New York Times* (over 5,000 separate articles, dating from the late 1930s to 1971) and Dwight Newton of *The San Francisco Examiner* (1949 to the present). To complete my overview of newspaper criticism, I also read the television reviews of two other senior newspaper critics—Lawrence Laurent of *The Washington Post* and Cecil Smith of *The Los Angeles Times.*

Besides this review of major critical writings on American television, I devised two comparative surveys which should help to reveal the general critical standards (and deficiencies) of writing about television. In the first survey, I wrote in mid-1975 to the television writers of 25 of the country's leading daily newspapers and the two major wire services, enclosing a chronological list of some 200 television "events" since 1948 which they, or their predecessors, had probably written about: the first shows of significant or popular series, various "specials," one-time dramas or documentaries, important live-event coverage, and major controversies. Unfortunately, few of these TV writers had kept copies or clippings of their reviews over the years—or perhaps they lacked the time to ferret them out for an unknown researcher. In any case, I managed to obtain at least a respectable sampling of additional articles by TV critics in Chicago, Denver, Garden City (N.J.), Indianapolis, Milwaukee, New York, St. Louis, San Diego, and the UPI.

My second survey was designed to judge television criticism by the standards applied to other fields. Television has often presented adaptations of works originally written for other media (Shakespeare, opera, feature films, etc.) and the work of writers and directors who have performed in other fields (Chayevsky, Frankenheimer, Lumet, Penn). Together, these provide the student of television criticism with a good opportunity to compare *its* standards with those applied to the same work or creator in other fields. How did the television critics' reviews of the original "Days of Wine and Roses" or "Marty" compare with film critics' reviews of the subsequent movie versions? Is an opera—the U.S. premiere of a Bernstein or Menotti work, for example—reviewed more generously or less knowledgably when presented on TV than when presented on the stage? Are Frederick Wiseman's documentaries judged differently on the box than in the cinema?

The Job of the TV Critic

Television (as its reviewers have often pointed out) is "everything." It includes not only almost all the other arts (drama, film, music, dance, visual design of many sorts), but also various forms of journalism. In this latter role, it is expected to cover local, national, and international politics; wars and disasters, presidential speeches, inaugurations, and national funerals; and almost anything else that passes as a news event. It also presents popular sports, classes (at many levels and in many subjects), intellectual (and non-intellectual) discussion, quiz shows, game shows, and other diversions; and innumerable advertisements. It is a complex, profitable, and much-regulated industry. It is an even more complex technology.

The TV columnist, reporter, reviewer, or critic would ideally be able to write intelligently about all of these things. Of those I have read so far, a handful have risen respectably well to the challenge: John Crosby (*The New York Herald-Tribune*), Marvin Kitman (*Newsday*), and John Leonard (*Life*, then *Newsweek*)—all three humorists at least as much as critics; in recent years, Ron Powers of *The Chicago Sun-Times*, Norman Mark of *The Chicago Daily News*, and Dwight Newton of *The San Francisco Examiner* (at least on Sundays) along with three or four other daily reviewers; Neil Compton of *Commentary*, Robert Lewis Shayon of *Saturday Review*, and —the reigning master of this unrespected craft—Michael Arlen of *The New Yorker*.

One problem is that most "television critics" in this country are obliged to spend a great deal of their time writing things other than criticism. They write news of the networks and gossip and features about television personalities. They write of legal and economic matters, audience surveys, pressure groups, sponsors, and ratings. Many of them are also responsible for assembling program logs and doing other journalistic chores far removed from what is generally thought of as criticism. In fact, much of the low repute of television writing in American newspapers is based on the assumption that the writer's work is often not criticism at all, but oblique publicizing— a mere assembling and editing of producers' press releases.

Even the relatively independent television writers, whose work is more highly esteemed than that of most daily reviewers, do a great deal of writing that is not focused on a specific program or series. Television, by its very nature, cries out for critical analysis as a social institution, no less than advertising, public schools, comic books, or the two-party system. Television is, in the language of the 1974 Aspen conference, a very potent "social and cultural force."

Over a few months in 1971, Robert Lewis Shayon of the *Sat-*

urday Review (now professor at the Annenberg School of Communications in Philadelphia) dedicated articles to the Fairness Doctrine, the effects of TV violence on children, racism on Alabama ETV, closed-circuit TV, license-renewal challenges, minority programming, advertising on children's television, and other issues more appropriately called media news than television criticism. The most thoughtful people in this country who have written about television with any regularity have addressed themselves to such subjects frequently and provocatively, just as Pauline Kael has speculated on the effects of movie violence and Eric Bentley has discussed the social-realistic pretensions of Broadway plays.

Beyond this onerous obligation to write about "everything," there are a few other considerations that make television criticism—especially daily television criticism—very nearly unique:

(1) Reviewers in most fields are expected to serve not only as aesthetic judges but also as reporters and, to some degree, as historians. But the peculiarities of television make these latter roles especially important for its critics. Students of criticism belittle the "trade-reporter's role" which most newspaper TV editors are obliged to fulfill. But given the defensive arrogance of the television industry, and the thick wadding of public relations and special-interest pressures in which the industry often wraps its activities, some American TV writers (Jack Gould, Norman Mark, Robert Lewis Shayon, Dwight Newton, and the *Variety* staff come to mind) have done a very good job of reporting indeed, and it is useful to us all that they have done it.

But good reviewing is also a form of reporting—perhaps that before anything else. In the case of television (like film, dance, and art), reviewing is the attempt to recreate in words a primarily nonverbal experience. Regarded absolutely, this is an impossible task, but the challenge should appeal to good writers. Instead of rising to it, however, too many television critics of the past generation have settled either for plus-or-minus adjectives pasted onto opaque plot summaries, or for verbal screens and polemic smoke that camouflage altogether the televised event.

In the years before regular network previewing, a standard lament of daily television reviewers was that they were always obliged to print their reviews after a program had been broadcast and, hence, could be of little real service to the viewer. Apart from the fact that most concert reviewers are in exactly the same position, I think this complaint makes sense only if one regards criticism as nothing more than consumer reporting.

After-the-fact reviews of unique performances (and most American television programs, remember, are still units in a series) can serve a valuable *educational* function. If you have already witnessed an event, a subsequent reading of a good critic's analysis is likely to enlarge and illuminate your own remembered experience, to recall aspects of it out of decaying or unconscious memory, to reveal possibilities of coherence, purpose, meaning, and beauty that can then become your *own* convictions. I came across one recreation of an Ed Murrow "Small World" program by John Lardner (*The New Yorker*, April 18, 1959) which was so convincing that I honestly thought I had seen it.

The evocative, exact descriptive critique can give readers who have not seen a program a keen sense of what took place—the journalistic function. Such reviews can also serve future students of American television, who will have to depend considerably on TV reporters and critics to discover what actually went out over the air during TV's first 25 years—the historical function.

It is probably just as well that most critics don't think of themselves as indispensible historians, but they are—or at least, like other journalists, they are the daily chroniclers on whose reports historians will depend. My own "collected sets" of Jack Gould, Dwight Newton, Cecil Smith, and Lawrence Laurent—plus the bound volumes of *TV Guide* from 1953 on—aren't the easiest things in the world to read through. But in the shocking absence of any consultable archive of *actual* past television programs, they compose an indispensable resource and tell a story quite different in its emphasis, thoroughness, standards, and details from works like Erik Barnouw's *History of American Broadcasting*.

(2) The sheer quantity of available American television forces a very demanding job of discrimination on the reviewer. Although previews and videotape recording devices now make it possible for the critic to view two or more programs broadcast at the same time, he still must choose *what* to criticize out of mountains of material. (TV producers and their publicists, of course, are always ready and willing to help the reviewers make their choices.)

(3) The series or serial structure of most American television, the daily repetition of news and talk shows, and the use of reruns and old movies present a frustrating challenge rarely dealt with satisfactorily by most television writers. While most TV viewers perceive television as an event of daily/weekly recurrence, the

critics, in general, discuss television programs as discrete, one-time-only happenings: the first show of a new series, the "special," the unique drama, documentary, or televised real-world event.

(4) Along the same lines, few television critics "use" television in the same way their readers do. The TV critic is on the look-out for novelty, quality, controversy, the new and different (as, to a degree, is the Broadway playgoer or the art gallery habitue). The average lay television viewer, on the other hand, opts for relaxing diversion, familiar faces, a reassuring sameness—the very things the networks know so well how to provide, but which can drive the intelligent critic up the wall, or back to books.

The critic-reader relation in limited circulation, "quality" magazines (*Commentary, The New Republic, The New Yorker*) may be different from this, but I wonder. Few critics seem able to accept, or deal with, the relatively uncritical casualness with which even their discriminating readers make use of TV. (An exception may be the occasional use of the "domestic drama" type of review. In this format, the reviewer tells us about his spouse, his children, his household routine—all as facetious pretext for commenting on the programs they watched last night. This intimate, chatty format has never been utilized, to my knowledge, by critics in any other field.)

(5) There are worlds of difference between the working conditions of the TV editor of a large daily newspaper, the television critic of a weekly or monthly magazine (who may be asked to contribute to only occasional issues), and the intellectual who offers his thoughts on television in a single essay or book. The daily TV critic (whose work is typically subject to the greatest amount of outside abuse) works under an extraordinary set of pressures his more leisured counterparts know nothing of: daily deadlines, 600-word limits, the obligation to fit a paper's existing style, Newspaper Guild regulations, publishers' hiring habits, and the pressing expectations of hundreds of thousands of local readers to be informed regularly on new shows, new seasons, new stars, and current issues.

The television critic of a newspaper, or even a lower-circulation magazine, also finds himself subject to the "outside" pressures of passionate reader mail, an avalanche of press releases, special previews and junkets, the demands of station-owning publishers and irate congressmen and community leaders, and the countless daily personal phone calls and visits from TV performers and executives. All of this occurs on a scale undreamed of by the TV critics' freer, perhaps more fortunate colleagues responsible for classical music, live drama, books, or art. Only popular music and the movies—two other tightly centralized, billion-dollar industries—visit similar pressures on their regular critics. No one can write about television for very long without becoming cognizant of and influenced by questions of "power."

The Power of the TV Critic

The television critics of America—whether alone, together, or through the agency of others—*do* have a certain degree of power over programming. This is one reason why it would be to our advantage to have good television critics. TV programmers and producers *have* sometimes changed their ways in response to published criticism, although never to the degree they have reacted to ratings. People hostile to critics—usually performers who are criticized—enjoy pointing out how frequently the public disagrees with them. Most television reviewers I have read disliked Milton Berle from the start, when he was attracting three-quarters of the viewing audience. On the other hand, they devoted a great deal of favorable attention to documentaries and cultural programs that drew what were for television relatively small audiences.

In television, as in other fields, a single critic can rarely "make or break" a show or a performer. However, a particularly strong writer, backed by some display of public opinion (or an obvious consensus of critical opinion), *can* affect the shape of television programming in the long run. Individual instances of "critical power" are difficult to isolate, since so many other factors enter into programming decisions. A few cases do come to mind; but in most of them there has been a *third* party involved between critic and network—a third party who was both more sensitive to reasoned, nonmonetary argument than most television executives, and more directly influential than the television critic.

For example, certain television writers argued for years that a well-supported, noncommercial American network was the only way out of the eternal cycle of lowest common denominator programming on the three advertiser-dominated chains. But it was only by means of the more powerful agencies of the Ford Foundation, the Carnegie Commission on Educational Television, and, ultimately, the U. S. Congress that the critics can be said to have "brought about" the Public Broadcasting System. Similarly, the Massachusetts-based pressure group called Action for Children's Television, which has played a crucial intermediary role in reforming children's programming *may* have been partly stimulated into existence by years of columns on the subject by critics like Robert Lewis Shayon. NBC has doubtlessly been cheered by 20 years of almost automatic praise from most reviewers for the offerings of its occasional "Hallmark Hall of Fame." But my suspicion is that this praise was even more important to J. C. Hall, the president of the program's sponsoring company, who wanted support and acknowledgement for what he regarded as his own important (and costly) contributions to American culture.

The favorable notice usually given in newspaper columns to news-documentaries, from "Victory at Sea" to the latest "CBS Reports," and to the more popularly oriented educational or NET/PBS fare (from "Shakespeare on TV" to "Upstairs/Downstairs") have no doubt attracted great numbers of viewers to these programs who would never otherwise have watched them. A consensus, or "ganging-up" of TV writers has also been given credit for the repeated showings of certain TV dramas; or for the extended lifetimes of certain popular but insufficiently profitable series ("Father Knows Best," "Mr. Peepers," "I Remember Mama," "The Voice of Firestone"); or for keeping others alive by promoting syndicated, non-network sales ("Lassie," "Star Trek," "The Lawrence Welk Show"). Often, the critics won these battles by marshalling letter-writing campaigns from their readers. But such successes (for what they're worth) have never been more than temporary, and they have been greatly outnumbered by the failures, particularly in recent years. In the earlier years of television, local station managers (who perhaps felt more uncertain than they do today of "what the viewer wants") seemed to respond more acutely to criticism in their local press.

Good Critics in Bad Times

Television criticism needs well-informed, independent men and women of taste, men and women who are also good writers possessed of a broad background of cultural reference and some sense of social responsibility. Within very broad ranges, I do think one can make certain value distinctions in TV criticism: between the Uninformed and the Well-Informed; the Well-Written and the Ill-Written; the Coherent and the Incoherent. (One might also risk the Useful and the Less Useful, the Original and the Unoriginal, the Fair and the Unfair—but then we would have to ask: useful to whom? original to whom? fair to whom?)

Even my minimal list is of dubious value. I can imagine (if not lay my hands on) a piece of criticism that was ill-informed, ill-written, and incoherent, and yet still valuable and useful; because, let us say:

— it was lit up here and there by flashes of real insight or provocative thought, like a bad opera with one or two great arias.

— its clumsiness and incoherence were the authentic marks of a real and rugged effort to come to terms with difficult material, as opposed to the slickly packaged wit of many pros.

— its misinformation was simply the mark of a beginner who may be looking freshly and newly, as opposed to the tediously encyclopedic knowingness of the jaded professional.

This leaves one with almost no standards of better or worse criticism, and (abstractly, theoretically) I almost believe there are none. Plus-or-minus judgment is certainly no test. Wise men disagree radically about almost every event in the world of art and entertainment.

You can get literary-elitist, or academic-philosophical (or whatever other model you happen to admire), and position television critics accordingly on your ladder of excellence. The usual way to do this is to name a critic from some other field who has obtained satisfactory credentials—James Agee or Andre Bazin or Penelope Houston or Pauline Kael, Vasari or Winckelmann or Ruskin or Clement Greenberg, Dr. Johnson or Ste. Beuve or the Schlegels or Alfred Kazin—and then measure television critics against your choice. Do that, however, and I don't think you'll come up with anyone who appears to "measure up"—who writes as well, thinks as deeply, brings to bear such a broad ground of cultural reference and specific knowledge and insight, whose writing is likely to prove as enduring—with the possible exception of Michael Arlen.

Television as a Cultural Force

American television—so far—has simply not been able to attract that kind of critic. The reasons usually given for this failure are the low status of the TV writer in any newspaper hierarchy; the claim that only a third-rate mind could willingly devote so many hours a week, year after year, to such a third-rate medium; the obligation to involve oneself so stickily with the shoddy thinking and vulgar values of network executives, TV actors, and agency men; and the refusal of broadly educated people to give to television the time they believe it is essential to give to other things—books, films, theater, music, conversation, and the world outdoors.

The three best-known and most influential sources of "journalistic," or regular, criticism of the arts and culture of the United States are *The New York Times*, *The New Republic*, and *The New Yorker*. It is for these three periodicals that a majority of the most-cited theatre, film, book, art, and music critics in this country have written. Each of these periodicals has also given considerable attention, if not always regular coverage, to the accomplishments and events of television.

For over 30 years, Jack Gould—directing, at his most influential, a staff of eight—reported for the *Times* on the intricate maneuvers and manipulations of the growing world of broadcasting. Employing the dogged, multi-column detail one expected of the *Times*, Gould was clearly more at home investigating and reporting, rather than reviewing. He lived in the *Times'* own special world of politics, money, and power, giving readers blow-by-blow, word-for-word accounts of the transfer of Channel 13 or of FCC hearings. He hectored and lectured the networks in thickset, avuncular prose, playing monitory moralist to the Sixth Avenue moguls. He was politically liberal and culturally conservative, forever counseling reason and the Middle Way.

When Gould retired, his reporting role was taken over by Les Brown of *Variety*. Brown is perhaps the one person in the country best-equipped to do the job properly, but he has none of Gould's "Golden Age" staff and is left to cover the gigantic TV newsbeat almost single-handedly. John J. O'Connor's appointment to fill the other half of Gould's role, as TV *critic*, marked a distinct improvement in this function. O'Connor writes better, thinks more interestingly, and seems less committed to television-as-it-is. On the whole, however, he seems hesitant to judge and fits in perhaps too easily with the *Times'* unexciting gallery of careful, relatively unadventurous critics past and present, all of whom have been read by producers with an attention beyond their due.

Eight different men have written about television at one time or another for *The New Republic*: Saul Carson, John Cogley, John Gregory Dunne, David Ebbitt, Paul Goodman, Walter Goodman, Roger Rosenblatt, and Reed Whittemore. Each had something sound and distinctive to offer, along the magazine's liberal-critical line. The best writer among them was probably Reed Whittemore ("Sedulus"), but already his collected columns seem as dated (and sometimes as clever) as John Crosby's of the '50s. There is about them something of the tone of the elder pedagogue trying to relax, without total success. Reading his columns alongside Stanley Kauffmann's film reviews (where they were usually run) is an embarrassing reminder of the different levels of criticism the two fields have attracted.

Before Michael Arlen, *The New Yorker* offered Philip Hamburger, a predictable middlebrow entertainer; John (son of Ring) Lardner, who often said useful things well; and, in two reviews each, Renata Adler (on game shows and the Children's Television Workshop) and Jonathan Miller, who wrote one supremely witty "anti-television" essay so deftly, almost madly turned that one excuses it for saying so little. I apologize for quoting at such length, but Miller is irreducible as well as unique:

> Television is a vast, phosphorescent Mississippi of the senses, on the banks of which one can soon lose one's judgment and eventually lose one's mind. The medium itself is depressing. The shuddering fluorescent jelly of which it's made seems to corrode the eye of the spectator and soften his brain. In television, the bodies and faces, the dances and games are suspended in a coldly glowing magma that must surely be repulsive to the touch: at once palpable and intangible—quite uncanny. It is like ectoplasm, in fact, which makes the term "medium" doubly appropriate. Television is a low-grade domestic seance in endless session, and the set goes to it with a vengeance, mouthing its gobbet of luminous cheesecloth until the tube burns out . . . Telly is a mean, fidgeting irritant, far smaller than one's own field of vision, flickering away in the corner of the eye like a dull, damaged butterfly. It would be mad, and certainly unfair, to expect consistent marvels from such a mingy little electronic membrane as

159

this. Not to mention all the other drawbacks of the instrument—the frame rolls, the flickers, the snowstorms, the ghosts, the warps, the jumps, the judders, the chronic vibrato. Not to mention the commercials which inhabit the crevices of the programs like vile, raucous parasites, jumping out all over the living room, nipping, tweaking, and chattering unforgivably about joints, armpits, skin wrinkles, bowels, and blocked-up nasal passages. And not, furthermore, to mention the way in which Telly slithers into the home and stays in one corner of the room like a horrible electronic gossip. In the suggestive gloaming of the darkened parlor, Telly is just one of a number of bits of furniture vaguely discerned in the general moonglow.

The Exception: Michael Arlen

I'm pleased that a man like Michael Arlen (who took over at *The New Yorker* late in 1966, three years after Miller gave up) has chosen to write essays on American culture as reflected on the cathode-ray tube. I'd be happy if a few more writers of such breadth and verve and originality gave it a try. (Few "higher thinkers" or good writers seem able to endure regular reporting on television for more than a few years. On retiring from the job, John Crosby said, "I can't sit and stare at that box for another ten years. I'd go crazy.") Arlen has been able to crack open new ways of thinking about television, as James Baldwin was able to do with our thinking about American racism in the 1950s, by writing freshly and honestly about subjects with which everyone is familiar.

Beginning on October 1, 1966, Arlen wrote 36 biweekly essays for *The New Yorker*, later collected in *Living-Room War*. He stopped in September 1968, to write three distinguished books on other subjects: *Exiles*, *An American Verdict*, and *A Voyage to Ararat*. Arlen returned to the subject of television in *The New Yorker* at the end of 1974.

The variety of his writing projects over such a relatively short time suggests that Arlen, like other intelligent TV critics (Mannes, Leonard, Crosby, Goodman) is really a *writer* first, dedicated to the examination of self and society through the instrument of a highly personal style. The seriousness of his dedication to the phenomenon of television—while he is working on it—is beyond ques-

tion: no critic in TV's short history comes close to the intensity
of his scrutiny, the depth of his insight, or the marvels of his style.
But for almost all fine minds who have tried to deal with American
TV on a regular, critical basis, the subject seems to wear thin, or to
exhaust the critic's patience, after a few months or years.

Arlen's superiority results, I think, from four things: his understanding of television, his "higher-critical" approach, his liberated
responses, and his fine style:

(1) His radical understanding of how American television works
has equaled or exceeded that of the most experienced TV reporters.
He is fully aware of its financial power structure, its manipulation of
politics, its cultural timidity, its over-readiness (before Watergate) to
serve as a propaganda arm to the government. He observes, times,
counts, telephones, and researches like the responsible journalist he
wishes TV newsmen would try harder to be. But he also responds,
emotionally and aesthetically, to TV *as TV*—not as a text with
background illustrations.

> They spent most of the time, really, on what Reagan said
> and what people were saying about Reagan—speeches and
> interviews, dull stuff. They did it filmically, though, cut-
> ting and panning, but cutting and panning in terms of the
> material, not in terms of what some art director thought
> was sexy, and the result was that it wasn't dull at all.

He can even explain convincingly why "Batman" is better television
than "Captain Kangaroo."

(2) From the start, Arlen had no particular interest in merely
reviewing "TV-as-programs." ("What is one going to say about
'Petticoat Junction' anyway—beyond making a few arch, superior
little cultural leaps in the air, and then jumping on its stomach?")
His real concern was rather for TV "as something we are doing to
ourselves." Generically speaking, this represents a quantum leap
toward a kind of "meta-criticism" of the Mailer/Kael variety, a leap
that a few architecture-environment critics are taking as well.

> A great many people obviously want the companionship
> of other voices as they pass through the day, with a sort
> of undemanding background picture thrown in to certify
> that the voices really exist as people . . .

> On the surface, television now gives us isolated facts. Some fun. Even, now and then, a tiny morsel of the world. But what it mostly gives us is some *other* world, the world we dream we live in. It tells us nothing, almost *nothing* about how life is and how we are . . .

This "higher criticism" reached a peak of indispensable insight into "television's reality" in a long 1968 essay ("Television and the Press in Vietnam," *Living-Room War*) that is the wisest thing I have ever read on television news.

(3) Arlen is blessed by a cynical liberation from kneejerk critical responses—especially to the kind of "liberal" pretentiousness that the networks (including the noncommercial network) purvey in their pompous self-defenses and proudly emit over the air in their "serious" programming. An obvious 1950s-style message play or an irresponsible piece of liberal propaganda in the guise of a documentary elicit from Arlen far more venomous contempt than does mere mediocrity.

(4) Arlen's is a fluid, manic, mercurial style, sometimes brash and colloquial ("Come off it, NBC!"). He has a helpless tendency to wit of a wild and airy kind that *can* run to drunken excess: there are novelistic fantasias and Tom Wolfeish montages that lose me altogether. Sentences dash and comma on, with breathless self-qualifying doublebacks (ho!) and repeats—piling up, shifting tone, accreting serio-comically along. There's a dilly in the great Vietnam piece that sparks and leaps on for 190 words. This critic is not writing for Everyman.

Rarely is Arlen's language mere style or self-expression, however. The anti-network ironies can have a savage directness. His near-surrealistic, semi-colloquial style seems to me akin to TV itself, which Arlen likes best when it is being its free, visual self, not some strained imitation of literature. *My* kind of English cannot do justice to most television; Michael Arlen's can. This is vanguard criticism; an intensely alert and mobile mind, armed with appropriate rhythms and diction, taking the phenomenon of American TV with total seriousness.

The eight essays of his I have read since his 1974 return are for the most part serious, well-reasoned critiques. Most valuable are several radical assessments of the format and judgments of TV network news, which Arlen finds depressingly unchanged over the eight-year gap in his TV writing—no more responsible as journalism, no more representative of reality now than then, no better a contribution to reasoned political judgment.

But something vital is missing from these later essays: the wit, the freedom, the freakiness have virtually disappeared. There are a few flings at the "Old Arlen," and one attempt to find new meanings in the communications explosion. But much of the 1974-75 writing reminds one of the older defenders of fairness, reason, and responsibility-to-viewers—a worthy enough standard, but one Arlen far outreached in 1966-68. He praises "The Adams Chronicles" as a worthy venture in Bicentennial nationalism, and argues for more foreign correspondents in TV news. He honors Frederick Wiseman in the kind of inflated, predictable tones the younger Arlen would, I think, have surely and cynically mocked: "It's a fascinating film —in some ways frightening, and also humorous, and dealing, albeit indirectly, with questions as deep as the modern soul." "The modern *soul*," Michael? "Albeit"? "Thus, today, in the new year of 1975, we are ensnared as never before in the overseas world, and involved at least as much as ever before with our fellow man . . ." Shayon? Gould? Your local congressman?

The Average TV Critic

Michael Arlen was, though—and he may be again—our best. But to ask for a battalion of Arlens would be silly. For one thing, you can't cook up critics to taste: They come when they're needed, where they're needed, and serve the audiences who need them. For another, the sort of television critics *most* people need—the men and women who would serve television and its viewers reasonably well— are non-intellectuals: decent writers with open minds, active consciences, a broad range of tastes, and an accessibility to at least some of what Pauline Kael happily calls "trash." They are people who *like* to watch television, as do most of their readers. And they aren't writing for *The New Republic* or *The New Yorker*, for *Commentary* or *Atlantic*.

I started my long trek through the newspaper columns dismayed by the trivia, bothered by the gossip, the journalese, the easy put-downs and puffs, the predictable "standards." But the more I read, the more I found myself realizing that this writing was more *like* television-as-it-is: it wasn't fighting it. Perhaps these *were* the right people to be writing about most television, both when it was good and when it was bad. They struck me as journalists closer to sports writers than to drama critics—but doesn't that make some kind of sense? Gossip about stars *belongs* to the world of television, as do slick eight-inch columns, written under pistol-to-the-head deadlines. There's a correspondence, an aptness between form of object and form of critique that is missing in most magazine reviewers. As one of Britain's keenest TV reviewers (Clive James of *The Observer*) recently wrote, "Criticism which does not reflect the medium's ephemerality and multiplicity (which are aspects of each other) is lying."

One doesn't want to push this idea too far. Dull, trivial subjects need not call forth only dull, trivial criticism. There have been good critics in bad times, like George Bernard Shaw and James Agee, who were able to spin straw into gold. Still, it is a lazy professional writer who cannot find *some* subject in television—be it a program, a person, or an issue—worthy of his serious attention once a day.

What troubles me most in the daily reviewers I have sampled is not so much their opinions or ideas as the quality of their prose. Too often, their prose seems to be mindlessly spun out of Winchellese jargon and fruity old metaphors and cliches. People who write so gracelessly and carelessly cannot, I believe, think very well. Perhaps they are (as other newsmen have claimed) mainly incompetent ex-reporters who couldn't handle more substantial assignments. In any case, I was dismayed to find that the men who run many of America's large daily newspapers allow such poor and apparently unedited prose to get through.

Attempts at a style loftier than this norm usually fell into one of three categories:

(1) Self-preening gags (See how clever I am?) and obvious phrase-making wit.

(2) Routine, ritual praise of Programs of Pretension. A collection of the American reviews of Shakespeare on TV, from Charlton Heston in *Julius Caesar* to Richard Chamberlain in *Hamlet*, would be an embarrassing display of ignorant awe.

(3) Pompous sermonizing over responsibility and taste, as if in imitation of Jack Gould at his most preach-

erly. In papers more provincial than the *Times*, this often takes the form of a smug, lowbrow conservatism, forever carping over necklines, long hair, or Suggestive Situations. There is a certain amount of timid crowd-pleasing in this category of reviewing. Many writers for the daily press seem hesitant to commit themselves on "breakthrough" series like "Laugh-in," "All In The Family," or "Mary Hartman, Mary Hartman" until they have read the ratings. Similarly, reviews of some particularly sentimental dramas appear to be contrived with a finger on the public pulse. In general, however, I think that America's television reviewers share, rather than lead or shape, America's tastes, and that their frequent professions of disgust or of unashamed tears are probably sincere. They *did* hate the Beatles, and David Brinkley, and PBL; they *do* love the Waltons.

Millions of Americans dote on their "own" daily TV reviewers, for all their dismal prose and timid taste, as they never could with critics of a wiser, keener stamp. The public see their tastes reflected in print, and they respond with comfort and fellow-feeling. Reviewers write to them personally, cosily, in chatty, daily letters about programs and stars—and they write back, tens of thousands of them, every week. Let it be.

I said earlier that the Useful/Useless, Original/Unoriginal, Fair/Unfair distinctions were dubious ones, dependent on the person using the criticism (what's useful/original/fair to *me* may not be to you). But let me venture one personal, non-absolute criticism of the critics. There is one category of TV criticism—and it fills the books and magazines—that I *do* regard as virtually useless and tediously unoriginal. Moreover, it is generally unfair, since it is unrepresentative or undescriptive of the object. This category is what I would call "anti-television" cant—the stringing together of more or less witty insults, usually in the form of metaphors for refuse ("garbage," "trash," "scum," "wasteland"), accompanied by standard, meaningless adjectives ("utter," "unmitigated," "absolute," "total," etc.). This, I think, gets nobody anywhere.

Such criticism is nondescriptive—it doesn't tell the reader anything about what was seen. It is, obviously, non-analytic. It is culturally condescending, an *expression* rather than a statement of disgust—and, even then, it is often only stock-response disgust, not disgust of the real and passionate sort. At best, it can only amuse by its surface of spleen (a trivial goal) and form a loose, snobbish bond between the critic and other unthinkingly anti-television types among his or her readers.

Standards for Good Television Criticism

The full potential of television communication is unlikely ever to be realized, or even explored, unless independent and imaginative thinkers take the time and effort to consider critically what television has done and, even more important, what it *might* have done. It would be helpful to us all if so influential, so culture-determining a thing as television were to be looked at closely and thought about carefully by a lot of intelligent people. The fact that most television programming to date may seem vapid and uninteresting (or worse) may be an excuse for ignoring it. But it is not, I think, a wholly adequate one. Television is now at least as essential a force as formal education in shaping this country's culture, and it is a considerably more essential force than the art one finds in galleries and museums—two subjects good critics are all too happy to keep writing about. Television is too important to be left to its market researchers and "creative" insiders—or to second-rate reviewers. After 25 years, American intellectuals wake up to discover that the world around them has been radically re-ordered by this vulgar, lowbrow toy. Disgusted by what they see, they rail as eloquently and futilely at television as earlier generations of thinkers railed at radios and cars. It will no longer do.

What should a *good* television critic do? The TV columns of the daily press have traditionally played several roles. They have served as consumer directories ("What to Watch Tonight"); as oblique letters of advice to producers and performers; as platforms for witty verbal display; and as genial conduits and translators of reader opinion. These roles can be serviceable and entertaining. But there are worthier uses, I think, to which television criticism can be put. Without either declining into routine, anti-television cant, or wafting into graceless, academic prose, the good television critic can serve several useful functions—quite apart from any considerations of his power to alter programming or change industry policy.

1. *The good television critic can point out lies, errors, and*

serious distortions when he discovers them in news and documentary programs. Most documentaries in the past 25 years have been reviewed by simply retailing to the reader the information presented by the producer, with no critical consideration of possible bias or inaccuracy. Such reviews could as easily be the networks' own press releases, and sometimes they are.

John J. O'Connor has remarked that network documentaries have become so predictable he no longer bothers to review them. Other TV critics ignore them because most of their readers do, or review them uncritically because they haven't the special competence to do anything more. But even "small" national evening ratings may represent millions of viewers, for whom TV news-documentaries—suavely packaged, predictably structured, and persuasive—may be the most vivid presentation of an issue that they will ever receive.

If the presentation is false, then surely someone (other than wounded special-interest groups) should be around to say so. And, "special competence," as any good reporter knows, can be developed in a very short time by diligent research into libraries, files, and public records, as well as by asking intelligent questions of people who know the answers. Norman Mark of *The Chicago Daily News* has done an exemplary job of testing the claims of documentaries by these means.

2. *The good critic can survey trends and types of programming over one or more so-called "seasons."* This would provide him with the opportunity not only to analyze the content of different programs and to make comparative evaluations, but also to suggest relationships between these changing forms and the world outside the box. It has become almost obligatory for a TV reviewer to count up and bewail the imitative excesses of this or that popular type of program at the beginning and end of each season (family situation comedies, variety shows, westerns, giveaway shows, detective shows, police shows, etc.). But one can do more than this. In the 1960s, Marya Mannes of *The Reporter* wrote two extended analyses of commercials and two others of daytime soap operas. They represent her wisest and most thoughtful work as a television critic.

Of all the critics I have read, however, only Neil Compton (*Commentary*, 1964-70) attempted serious critical surveys of genres, types, and categories of programs on any regular basis. He took popular culture with the proper degree of seriousness and understood the realities of TV production and TV viewing. He always watched a great deal of television carefully before he wrote, and then he produced cogent critical essays in which he surveyed individual program-types over a season: Vietnam documentaries, pop music shows, children's daytime cartoons. He was never taken in by "prestige" programming, which is generally more pretention than substance.

On the whole, I found Compton to be a civilized critical chronicler, responsible but never pontifical, who remained readable without ever depending on the thin surface-sparkle of "wit":

> Perhaps it is naive to expect a medium which offers a service as domestic as a picture window and as continuous as running water to duplicate the conventional forms of theater and cinema, which are based on an audience which chooses freely among alternatives and commits time, energy, and money to the act of participation. The vast, unbuttoned universality of the television audience and the ritualistic repetitiveness of the weekly schedule mean that empathy is achieved, if at all, only after a half-dozen or more installments of a series have established a cadre of habitual viewers. Why should any dramatist choose to write to such a medium so long as theater and movies are open to him? Almost without exception, the best television dramas have been adaptations of works originally conceived for other media: the tendency of popular TV programs generally to be "spin-offs" of movies, comic books, novels, or musical comedies is more than a matter of mere witless imitation. (*Commentary*, April 1966)

3. *The good critic should also, from time to time, venture radical considerations of the very nature and creative possibilities of the medium.* How, for example, might the size of the television screen, the quality of its image, and the domestic locus of viewing affect the *kind* of comic or serious drama written for television, or the methods of directing and acting it? Producers, I am sure, ask such questions. But critics have usually dealt with them only in infrequent asides tucked into the format of a standard program review.

4. *Rather than simply attending to and then evaluating what appears on the television set, the good critic might on occasion inquire into the phenomenon and the social effects of those television programs which have now become either national rituals, or materials*

that we have come to ingest as naturally and unconsciously as the air through which they are transmitted. Some examples might be the annual Academy Awards and similar galas; the Miss America (etc.) competitions; the quadrennial national nominating conventions of the Democratic and Republican parties; the long moonshot watches; the three nightly half-hour network news presentations, with their studio "anchormen" and stand-up correspondents "on location"; the TV family that acts out comic situations in three eight-minute scenes between commercials; the humorless, ill-drawn adventures of cartoon heroes on Saturday mornings; or (reaching back into history) such things as the charity telethons of the early 1950s.

Some of these forms have already been studied for their own sake—especially network news. John Lardner once speculated at length on the "adult western" of 1957, and Horace Newcomb has written a sound and provocative book (*TV: The Most Popular Art*) on the mythical imagery of various popular TV genres. The 1958-59 quiz show scandal provoked a small library of inquiries into national values, and a few critics have puzzled over the "misery show" marvel, or the fact and effects of "commercial interruptions."

In 1963, Paul Goodman wrote a series of eleven essays on TV for *The New Republic* and, in the process, proved himself to be one of the few authentically radical thinkers to have addressed themselves to the medium. Some of the issues he raised were shocking in their simplicity, but they had rarely been raised before. A sample:

> On election night . . . there is a most impressive coverage of the returns in the race between the two matched pacers, and TV takes pride in this democratic service, though it defeats me exactly how democracy is served by it, since before TV people always managed to find out anyway who was elected President.

Normally, the harried daily reviewer cannot be expected to do any more than accept such phenomena as "givens" and compare one with another. Which network covered the convention best? Which station has the most appealing anchorman? Was this year's Emmy Show worse than the last? Perhaps I am the only person in the country who still regards the fact of an unstructured, two-hour long "talk show," nationally telecast every night, as an event utterly without reasonable explanation. Twenty years after Jack Paar first walked into *Tonight*, it still strikes me as an event worthy of radical investigation. What is—and *why* is—a Talk Show?

Most daily TV reviewers can protest that their readers and their editors have been conditioned to expect more simple, easily digestible fare than what I am proposing. But the Sunday editions of *The Los Angeles Times* and *The Washington Post* (to say nothing of the quality press of London and continental Europe) have demonstrated that editors and readers can accustom themselves to serious critical essays, at least once a week.

5. *The good critic should certainly investigate the commonplace notion that many people now depend on television for their conception of (or accept television in lieu of) the real world.* What exactly does this mean? What are the implications of this claim? Television shares certain basic qualities with cinema—both are made up of "motion pictures," usually photographed images of real things, displayed on a two-dimensional, rectangular screen. As a medium, then, and also in its individual programs, television invites the kind of theoretical speculation into its nature that has attended the study of film by such critics as Arnheim, Bazin, Kracauer, and Metz. Our manner of perceiving television lies open to both philosophical enquiry and physiological experimentation. Like cinema, it has evolved certain stock forms and fostered certain stereotypes and myths. Hence, like cinema, it affords rich material for criticism along generic and mythic lines.

Insofar as television shares other characteristics with still photography and journalism (the representation of real events), it also invites other forms of theoretical and critical investigation. One might examine, for instance, the relationship between the reality supposedly captured and transmitted by television (the battle of Con Thien, the life of the Loud family) and the translation of that reality into television's images and sounds. A serious critic might further examine the differences between our *experience* of such actual events, and our experience of television's versions of them.

6. *What appears on American television is at once the product of and (in a fuzzy way) a reflection of American society: "a window on the world," in the words of Sonny and Cher. A social critic possessed of sufficient temerity and self-assurance might well make use of the medium of television criticism to discuss both that window and that world.* Some critics have done this in limited ways, but usually by means of critical comment on disagreeable peculiar-

ities they find in television itself. (Commercials and giveaways, for instance, are frequently seen as a "reflection" of American greed.)

But the brave television critic can go even farther than this. He can (as the greatest critics have always done) analyze the *subject presented* as well as the means of presentation. There is no reason —other than fear of one's publisher, or one's own lack of competence—*not* to write of the state of American politics (or music, or foreign policy, or health care) in the context of an essay on TV's coverage of an election campaign (or "NBC Opera," or "CBS Evening News," or an "ABC Closeup" on doctors). With the bravery of hindsight, I was appalled to find how few daily TV critics in 1954 felt free or willing or able to say anything about the Army-McCarthy hearings other than the hours they were visible on TV. In recent years, the television critic who has taken greatest advantage of this opportunity—to write about "everything" in the process of writing about television—is Michael Arlen, whose *New Yorker* essays on "The Living Room War" began with, but then reached far beyond, a discussion of the television reporting on the Vietnam War.

7. *Every good critic is potentially a teacher.* I take it as axiomatic that the good critic of a particular field (perhaps not on first hiring, but certainly after a few dozen critical assignments) (a) knows more about the field than most of his readers; (b) attends more closely than they to particular events and therefore is, in Henry James' phrase, "one of those people on whom nothing is lost"; (c) is better able than they to articulate his response. As a result of these three superiorities, the good critic can (a) teach his readers more about the field—its methods of production, institutional structures, external and internal pressures and limitations; (b) train them to be better receivers of the art, to be more sensitive, more critical, more alert, and more attentive to all the possible sources of pleasure or information; and (c) enable them to give definable mental and verbal shape to (and, hence, retain as a permanent asset) this enhanced personal response.

Toward a New Criticism

Most books, and many articles, written so far on American television have been sociology, not criticism. A critic may, and perhaps should, be aware of the best social scientific research in his field. But it is not his role to practice it. To attempt to assess objectively what other people think about TV, or how much they need it, or how it affects them, has nothing to do with the art and practice of criticism, which depends for its basic data on the *individual* response (what Eric Sevareid condescendingly calls "the egocentric exercise of analyzing [one's] own reactions").

I think we are seeing the beginning of a new criticism, dependent on a new sensibility perhaps partly *formed* by television. It is based on a rich yet exact, a free yet knowing use of the English language. Its practitioners are able to modulate easily from the traditional to the vernacular, from the personal to the analytic. It is as intelligent as it is liberated. It is the language of (at their best) Norman Mailer, the editors of *Rolling Stone*, Pauline Kael—and Michael Arlen. It is a sort of late twentieth century, educated-American-demotic, unique (as far as I know) in the history of the language, although reminiscent of some of the juicier Victorians (Arnold, Carlyle, Dickens).

Along with this new use of language goes a happy, unfettered willingness to experience and deal with "popular" subjects. By this, I don't mean the earnest analyses of the Bowling Green Professor of Popular Culture, whose language, stance, background, and very life are usually alien to the popular subjects he tries to elevate and ennoble by his attention. I don't mean skittery verbal entertainers like Tom Wolfe, culturally slumming in an artificial prose, or a Marshall McLuhan; or most of the clumsy, inexpressive rock music reviewers, who haven't one-tenth the mind or style or lucidity or *reach* of the people I am describing.

The writers I'm referring to are very bright people, aware of and excited by contemporary culture, but in vital contact with past history as well. They can seem almost magically creative and free, and yet they are careful and correct in their use of the language. I suspect, in fact, that it's their very self-assurance and skill with the language that allows them their extraordinary insights into the things they discuss. This would also explain their excesses, their over-the-cliff fantasies (Mailer, Kael, *Rolling Stone*, and Arlen are all prone to these), the times when they get carried away by their own verbal and imaginative virtuosity. They also seem to share a near-manic taste for chaos and disorder, which may explain why they are able to tune in so clearly to the times of which they write:

It isn't, perhaps, that the world is deeper in chaos than it used to be, but that the element of chaos which has always been there in life, which really *is* life . . . is now coming more and more out from under wraps.

My own feelings—my own feelings (he mumbled) are that the divinity of man was a rather nice thing while it lasted but that we are now all so well along on the road to a life of metal and organization and technique and cultural technology and educational technology and sexual technology and all the rest of the morbid paraphernalia of modern life that it will take a few exertions of nothing much less than a kind of anarchism of the soul (well, there's a floaty expression for you) to even postpone the desert for a while.

The Flying Nun is interrupting Dean Rusk? Dean Rusk is interrupting *The Flying Nun*? This country seems to include both, in some mysterious, lunatic balance, and television includes both too . . .   (Michael Arlen, *Living-Room War*)

Put to the question, I would depend for the "future of television criticism" not on the egoistic pontificators; not on sociologists, futurologists, or cultural slummers; not on the "Isn't TV Awful?" wits, or the people who Don't Like Television Except When It's Very, Very Good; not even on traditional intellectuals like myself. I would depend, rather, on the good men and women who *like* TV and use it as most people do—but who, in addition, write clearly, have consciences, and are willing to live with the realities of the daily press. I would also depend on Front-Line writers and thinkers of the sort I have just tried to describe. They're rare, but there will be more. Television, I think, is helping to create them.

Television as a Cultural Force: A Selected Reading List

Christopher H. Sterling

The following short annotated listing is restricted to book-length materials which are either currently in print, or likely to be found in a good library. Nearly all the material is devoted to American television, with just a few citations referring to British programs. Books felt especially useful are marked with an asterisk (*), while (P) indicates that the title is available in paperback form. The listing is somewhat arbitrarily divided into four sections: (1) television programming in general, (2) specific program case studies, (3) analyses of television news, and (4) collected television criticism.

Television Programming in General

Barnouw, Erik. *The Image Empire: A History of Broadcasting in the United States Since 1953.* New York: Oxford University Press, 1970. 396 pp. The third volume of Barnouw's social history. Deals with network television's increasing role in

---

Mr. Sterling edits *Journal of Broadcasting* and the monthly *Mass Media Booknotes*, and is associate professor of communications at Temple University in Philadelphia.

American life (though the author also goes into lengthy tangents on the role of American media abroad).

Barnouw, Erik. *Tube of Plenty: The Evolution of American Television.* New York: Oxford University Press, 1975. 518 pp. A single-volume summation of the television material contained in Barnouw's three-volume history, mainly from the book just above. Illustrated and brought up to date, but otherwise quite similar (see either this or the preceding book, but not both).

Berger, Arthur Asa. *The TV-Guided American.* New York: Walker, 1976. 194 pp. A popular culture approach to specific entertainment shows—and what each tells about its viewers.

Bower, Robert T. *Television and the Public.* New York: Holt, Rinehart & Winston, 1973. 205 pp. Results of a 1970 national audience survey on program preferences, viewing habits, and characteristics, providing comparisons with a 1960 survey (Steiner, *The People Look at Television,* 1963) and a good overview of TV's impact.

Brown, Les. *Televi$ion: The Business Behind the Box.* New York: Harcourt Brace Jovanovich, 1971. 374 pp. (P) A detailed, behind-the-scenes analysis of network program decision-making during 1970, concentrating on the factors behind the decisions and the people involved. One of the most revealing books around.

*Cantor, Muriel G. *The Hollywood Television Producer: His Work and His Audience.* New York: Basic Books, 1971. 256 pp. Author's Ph.D. dissertation and the only study of its type. Explores the job constraints and activities of prime-time program producers from a sociological perspective.

Cole, Barry G., ed. *Television: Readings from "TV Guide."* New York: Free Press, 1970. 605 pp. (P) Some 80 selections on all aspects of the medium, with pp. 119-282 devoted to various aspects of programming. Revised version due late in 1976.

*Federal Communications Commission (Office of Network Study). *Television Network Program Procurement.* Washington: FCC, 1963 (Part I), and 1965 (Part II). 494 and 838 pp. (P) Exhaustive analysis of a process that has changed little in the past decade. Based on extensive hearings, and including many quotations from testimony of network and package agency personnel on program decisions and content.

Glick, Ira, and Sidney J. Levy. *Living with Television.* Chicago: Aldine, 1962. 262 pp. Essentially a study of audience listening patterns. Deals with preferences in programming and types of listeners, thus giving a vast amount of data on programs.

Glut, Donald F., and Jim Harmon. *The Great Television Heroes.* New York: Doubleday, 1975. 245 pp. Short illustrated study written for the nostalgia market, and covering network programs up to about 1960. Discusses both children's and adult programs of various types, dealing with their characters and content trends.

*Head, Sydney W. *Broadcasting in America: A Survey of Television and Radio.* Boston: Houghton Mifflin, 1976 (3rd edition). 630 pp. Best single volume explaining American broadcasting, how it works, and how it got to be that way. Good starting point for those who lack background in the subject. Useful 50-page annotated bibliography as well.

*Kuhns, William. *Why We Watch Them: Interpreting TV Shows.* New York: Benziger, 1970. 209 pp. (P) Analysis of program genres and specific shows current at the time of publication, relating characters and plot to their appeal for viewers.

Mayer, Martin. *About Television.* New York: Harper and Row, 1972. 433 pp. (P) Broad discussion of the business with emphasis on program types and trends in commercial and public television, mainly on a national level.

Michael, Paul. *The Emmy Awards: A Pictorial History.* New York: Crown, 1971. 382 pp. Some 12-18 pages per year of photos, brief text, and analysis. Gives a sense of top network entertainment and news programs of each season.

*Newcomb, Horace. *TV: The Most Popular Art*. New York: Double-day Anchor Books, 1974. 272 pp. (P) Chapters divided along network program genre lines, covering both entertainment and information formats. Discusses content types and conventions with many examples from specific series and even specific episodes.

Owen, Bruce M., Jack H. Beebe, and Willard G. Manning, Jr. *Television Economics*. Lexington, Mass.: Lexington Books, 1974. 219 pp. Title is misleading, as most of book deals with programming and how economic factors affect it. Includes a good deal of tabular reference material along the way.

Settel, Irving, and William Laas. *A Pictorial History of Television*. New York: Grosset & Dunlap, 1969. 210 pp. More text than the two volumes below, but too episodic to be of much value. Again, the concentration is on programs and stars.

Shulman, Arthur, and Roger Youman. *How Sweet it Was: Television, a Pictorial Commentary*. New York: Shorecast, 1966 (several reprint editions). 448 pp. Now a decade old, but still the best pictorial history of network programming ever done.

Shulman, Arthur, and Roger Youman. *The Television Years*. New York: Popular Library, 1973. 322 pp. (P) Essentially the same material as the volume above, with some updating and re-arranged by year rather than program type. Mainly pictures.

Surgeon General's Scientific Advisory Committee on Television and Social Behavior. *Television and Social Behavior, Volume I: Media Content and Control*. Washington: Government Printing Office, 1972. 546 pp. (P) Some 300 pages on U.S. television programming as perceived by parents, the industry, and critics. Also, four long essays on program content and trends in four selected foreign countries.

Tuchman, Gaye, ed. *The TV Establishment: Programming for Power and Profit*. Englewood Cliffs, N.J.: Prentice-Hall, 1974. 186 pp. (P) Highly anti-establishment view of the networks, concentrating on programming and economic issues.

Williams, Raymond. *Television: Technology and Cultural Form.* New York: Schocken Books, 1975. 160 pp. (P) Useful structural analysis of what television is and does, focusing on the effects of technology on content and impact.

*Zettl, Herbert. *Sight, Sound, Motion: Applied Media Aesthetics.* Belmont, Calif.: Wadsworth, 1973. 401 pp. The best single guide to thinking visually in a medium (especially film and television). Extensively illustrated and containing many examples of how pictures and other media elements communicate different things.

Specific Program Case Studies

Blumenthal, Norman. *The TV Game Shows.* New York: Pyramid Books, 1975. 272 pp. (P) Popular discussion of program types, operations and economics, personalities, and details on network shows. Useful for "behind-the-scenes" approach even though aimed mainly at quiz show viewers.

Brodhead, James E. *Inside Laugh-In.* New York: Signet Paperback T4059, 1969. 159 pp. (P) The only fairly serious published study of how this once popular program developed and how a typical show was produced.

*Diamant, Lincoln. *The Anatomy of a Television Commercial.* New York: Hastings House, 1970. 190 pp. Illustrated album exploring all facets of production and use of a two-minute Kodak film ad. Only study of its type on a TV commercial.

Edmondson, Madeleine, and David Rounds. *The Soaps: Daytime Serials of Radio and TV.* New York: Stein & Day, 1973. 190 pp. A short and informal analysis with useful behind-the-scenes information on production.

Ellens, J. Harold. *Models of Religious Broadcasting.* Grand Rapids, Mich.: Eerdmans, 1974. 168 pp. (P) Useful and sometimes humorous analysis of the varied types of religious programs on the air and the people behind them.

*Elliott, Philip. *The Making of a Television Series: A Case Study in the Sociology of Culture*. New York: Hastings House, 1972. 180 pp. Analysis of a seven-part British television documentary, from conception of idea through development of script, cast and properties, and series production. Concentration throughout on the process of television program creation. Best study of its type to date.

*Gerrold, David. *The World of Star Trek* and *The Trouble with Tribbles*. New York: Ballantine Books, 1973. 278 and 275 pp. (P) Developed for the vast cult of believers in this network show. These two studies offer valuable views of the production process—the first volume looking at the whole program process, and the second volume reviewing a specific episode (Gerrold wrote the script).

Johnson, William O. *Super Spectator and the Electronic Lilliputians*. Boston: Little, Brown, 1971. 238 pp. The only lengthy study of television's effect on professional sports, and vice versa. Taken from articles in *Sports Illustrated*. Good data here on just how television manages to cover different types of sport events.

LaGuardia, Robert. *The Wonderful World of TV Soap Operas*. New York: Ballantine Books, 1974. 342 pp. (P) A light, fan-type book which offers some useful background and production information on the soaps, their characters, and creators as well as plot outlines.

Miller, Merle, and Evan Rhodes. *Only You, Dick Daring!* New York: Sloane, 1964. 350 pp. (P) Tongue-in-cheek, but an essentially true tale of an attempt to sell a program idea to then CBS Television President James Aubrey—and the reasons for this venture's failure. Useful analysis of program idea development problems.

*Stedman, Raymond William. *The Serials: Suspense and Drama by Installment*. Norman: University of Oklahoma Press, 1971. 514 pp. Scholarly yet eminently readable history of the serial form in film, radio, and television, the latter being one of the best available analyses of content and impact of this format.

*Whitfield, Stephen and Gene Roddenberry. *The Making of Star Trek*. New York: Ballantine Books, 1968. 414 pp. (P) Probably the best study of a commercial network program ever published. Recommended even for those who did not care for the program, as it provides detail on early conception of the idea, character and actor development, sets and props, writer guidelines, pilot production, etc.

Analyses of Television Journalism

*Barrett, Marvin, ed. *The Alfred I. DuPont-Columbia University Survey of Broadcast Journalism*. New York: Grosset & Dunlap 1969-71), Crowell (1972-date). (P) Originally an annual and now biennial. Offers the best overview of developments in both network and local television news and documentary production. Each year's volume has different main title.

*Bluem, A. William. *Documentary in American Television*. New York: Hastings House, 1965. 310 pp. Now badly dated (a revision is in preparation), but still the best single study of the development of the documentary format in TV, with brief discussion of film and radio antecedents.

Diamond, Edwin. *The Tin Kazoo: Television, Politics and the News*. Cambridge, Mass.: MIT Press, 1975. 269 pp. Discussion of the current place of television network news in American life with critical viewpoint. Suggests that TV has less impact now than it did in the past as audience is more sophisticated and used to visual conventions. Detailed discussion of major episodes in the Nixon vs. press battles.

Epstein, Edward Jay. *News From Nowhere: Television and the News*. New York: Random House, 1973. 321 pp. (P) Detailed analysis of the process of gathering and reporting the evening network news during the 1968-69 season, with discussion of the people, restrictions, decision-making, and the final product. Critical, and somewhat dated (based on author's Ph.D. dissertation).

Fixx, James F. (general ed.). *The Mass Media and Politics*. New York: *New York Times*/Arno Press, 1972. 636 pp. Facsimiles of *NYT* articles and reviews of political communication (especially broadcasting) from 1936 through 1971.

Gilbert, Robert E. *Television and Presidential Politics*. North Quincy, Mass.: Christopher Publishing, 1972. 335 pp. Coverage of television's effects on campaigning from 1952 through 1968 campaigns with details on varied uses of the medium.

LeRoy, David J., and Christopher H. Sterling, eds. *Mass News: Practices, Controversies, and Alternatives*. Englewood Cliffs, N.J.: Prentice-Hall, 1973. 334 pp. (P) Several articles (including some original here) on television newscasts and documentaries —and problems in creative production of both.

*MacNeil, Robert. *The People Machine: The Influence of Television on American Politics*. New York: Harper & Row, 1972. 262 pp. (P) A highly critical review of network television news methods and reporting, with emphasis on political coverage both in and after campaigns.

Mickelson, Sig. *The Electric Mirror: Politics in an Age of Television*. New York: Dodd, Mead, 1972. 304 pp. Former head of CBS News examines television coverage of national political campaigns and conventions.

Skornia, Harry J. *Television and the News: A Critical Appraisal*. Palo Alto, Calif.: Pacific Books, 1968. 232 pp. Detailed and scholarly study of several selected limitations on TV news— courtroom reporting, news blockage, commercial pressure, etc.

Small, William. *To Kill a Messenger: Television News and the Real World*. New York: Hastings House, 1970. 302 pp. (P) Head of CBS News in Washington discusses the industry's point of view on news and documentary problems with government and others.

Wood, William A. *Electronic Journalism*. New York: Columbia University Press, 1967. 175 pp. Broad overview of practices and impact a decade ago.

Yellin, David. *Special: Fred Freed and the Television Documentary.* New York: Macmillan, 1972. 289 pp. Interesting study of a long-time CBS and NBC producer (who died shortly after the book appeared), made even more interesting by Freed's own descriptions of his work and the production process.

Collected Television Criticism

*Adler, Richard, ed. *Television as a Social Force: New Approaches to TV Criticism.* New York: Praeger Special Studies, 1975. 171 pp. (P) The predecessor to the present volume, this includes eight original papers from a 1974 Aspen conference, taking a broader view of television's social role.

*Arlen, Michael. *Living-Room War.* New York: Viking Press, 1968. 242 pp. (P) Arlen's collected writings about television from his column in *The New Yorker*, examining television news and other subjects. Some of the best TV criticism done.

Crosby, John. *Out of the Blue: A Book about Radio and Television.* New York: Simon and Schuster, 1952. 301 pp. The collected work of the critic for the old *New York Herald Tribune.*

Ellison, Harlan. *The Glass Teat* and *The Other Glass Teat.* New York: Ace, 1970; New York: Pyramid, 1975. 317 and 397 pp. (P) Collected anti-establishment (and somewhat predictable) television criticism of the *Los Angeles Free Press* critic.

Hazard, Patrick D., ed. *TV as Art: Some Essays on Criticism.* Champaign, Ill.: National Council of Teachers of English, 1966. 160 pp. (P) Discussion of dramatic, musical, and other program formats in the arts.

*Newcomb, Horace, ed. *Television: The Critical View.* New York: Oxford University Press, 1976. 314 pp. (P) Twenty essays dealing with specific programs, program genres, the role of TV in society, and the aesthetics of television compared to other media and art forms.

*Schwartz, Tony. *The Responsive Chord.* New York: Doubleday, 1973. 210 pp. (P) Almost McLuhanesque discussion of the aesthetics of audio communication (including TV sound), especially in commercial and political advertising.

Seldes, Gilbert. *The Public Arts*. New York: Simon and Schuster, 1956. 303 pp. (P) The best statement on television programming by the one-time dean of media critics. For his earlier thinking on television, see *The Great Audience* (Viking, 1950).

Shayon, Robert Lewis, ed. *The Eighth Art: Twenty-Three Views of Television Today*. New York: Holt, Rinehart & Winston, 1962. 269 pp. Original essays on all aspects of television content. Originally assembled for a CBS quarterly that never appeared.

Shayon, Robert Lewis. *Open to Criticism*. Boston: Little, Brown, 1971. 324 pp. Unique self-analysis of the then-critic for *Saturday Review*. Includes many of his columns, the background of their writing, and his latest reaction to it all.

Sopkin, Charles. *Seven Glorious Days, Seven Fun-Filled Nights*. New York: Simon and Schuster, 1968. 241 pp. (P) One man's somewhat cynical report of a solid week of viewing the New York television channels (all seven of them)—what he saw and what he thought about what he saw.

White, David Manning, and Richard Averson, eds. *Sight, Sound and Society: Motion Pictures and Television in America*. Boston: Beacon Press, 1968. 466 pp. Collected writings and articles, about half on television, with a strongly critical tone.

Appendix

Workshop Meetings: New York—December, 1974
Berkeley—January, 1975
Chicago—March, 1975
Palo Alto—May, 1975
New York—May, 1975

Aspen Conference: July, 1975

RICHARD ADLER
Director
Aspen Television Workshop

ROBERT ALLEY
Department of Religion
University of Richmond

JOSEPH ANGELL
Fort Collins, Colorado

MARVIN BARRETT
Director
Columbia-Dupont Survey
Graduate School of Journalism
Columbia University

PETER BERGER
Department of Sociology
Rutgers University

AL BURTON
Director of Program Development
T A T Communications

ERNEST CALLENBACH
Editor
Film Quarterly

DOUGLASS CATER
Director
Aspen Institute Program on
    Communications and Society

CAROL CHRIST
Department of Religious Studies
Columbia University

CHARLES CLIFT
School of Radio-Television
Ohio University

DAVID CONNELL
Vice-President, Production
Children's Television Workshop

PEGGY COOPER
Assistant to the President
WTOP-TV
Washington, D.C.

MIDGE DECTER
Basic Books, Inc.

BENJAMIN DeMOTT
Department of English
Amherst College
Member, TV Workshop
    Steering Committee

EDITH EFRON
Television critic
New York

PAULA FASS
Department of History
University of California,
    Berkeley

GARY GILSON
Producer
WNET-TV, New York

JACK GOULD
Former television critic
New York Times

HANS GUTH
Department of English
California State University,
San Jose

ANDREW HACKER
Department of Political Science
Queens College
City University of New York

DAVID HALLIBURTON
Department of English
Stanford University

IRVING HARRIS
The Harris Group, Inc.
Chicago

JAMES HOGE
Editor
Chicago Sun-Times

JAMES KRAFT
National Endowment for
the Humanities

GERALD LESSER
Graduate School of Education
Harvard University

LESLIE LIPSON
Department of Political Science
University of California,
Berkeley

DAVID LITTLEJOHN
Graduate School of Journalism
University of California,
Berkeley
Member, TV Workshop
Steering Committee

DAVID MILLER
Department of Religion
Syracuse University

LYNN MILLS
Director
Prime Time School Television

JOHN B. MOORE
Department of Philosophy
Northwestern University

WILLIAM NESTRICK
Department of English
University of California,
Berkeley

DWIGHT NEWTON
Television critic
San Francisco Examiner

MICHAEL NOVAK
Chairman
TV Workshop
Steering Committee

JOHN O'CONNOR
Television critic
New York Times

AL PERLMUTTER
Vice President
News Documentaries
NBC News

KENNETH PIERCE
Editor
Columbia Journalism Review
Columbia University

NORMAN PODHORETZ
Editor
Commentary

ROGER ROSENBLATT
National Endowment for
the Humanities

JACK ROSENTHAL
New York Times

LUCIO RUOTOLO
Department of English
Stanford University

JOHN RUSSO
Department of English
University of Chicago

188

BARBARA RYAN
Television critic
Denver Post

KEVIN RYAN
Associate Dean
Ohio State University

STEVEN H. SCHEUER
TV Key
New York

ALEX SEGAL
Drama Division
University of Southern
 California

JOHN SISK
Department of English
Gonzaga University

DAVID SONTAG
Television producer and
 writer
Aspen, Colorado

SHARON SPERRY
Assistant Director
Poynter Center
Indiana University

BENJAMIN STEIN
Editorial Page
Wall Street Journal

CHRISTOPHER STERLING
School of Communications
Temple University

STUART SUCHERMAN
The Ford Foundation

FRANK SWERTLOW
Television writer
United Press International

WILLIAM VEEDER
Department of English
University of Chicago

PAUL WEAVER
Associate Editor
Fortune Magazine
Member, TV Workshop
 Steering Committee

DAVID WEBSTER
Director-United States
British Broadcasting Corporation

PETER WOOD
Department of History
Duke University

Index

ABOUT THE EDITORS

Richard Adler

Mr. Adler is assistant director of the Aspen Program and director of its Workshop on Television Criticism. He was formerly assistant professor of English at Oberlin College. Mr. Adler is co-editor (with Walter S. Baer) of the *Aspen Notebook: Cable and Continuing Education, The Electronic Box Office*, and (with Douglass Cater) *Television as a Social Force*. He is also serving as director of a program of research on the effects of television advertising on children at the Harvard Graduate School of Education.

Douglass Cater

Mr. Cater is founder of the Aspen Institute Program on Communications and Society and executive editor of the Aspen Program's Series on Communications. He is also consulting professor in Political Science and Communication at Stanford University.

From 1964 to 1968 he served as special assistant to President Lyndon B. Johnson, concentrating particularly on education and health programs. During this time, he worked on the shaping and passage of the Public Broadcasting Act of 1967. Before his White House assignment, he was the Washington and national affairs editor for *The Reporter* magazine and an associate director of Wesleyan's Center for Advanced Studies.

Mr. Cater received a Guggenheim Fellowship and an Eisenhower Fellowship and is the recipient of the George Polk Memorial Award and the "Harry" award for his contribution to public broadcasting. His other books include *Power in Washington, The Fourth Branch of Government, Ethics in a Business Society* (with Marquis Childs), and *TV Violence and the Child* (with Stephen Strickland).

The following titles have been published in cooperation with the Aspen Institute Program on Communications and Society:

ASPEN NOTEBOOK: Cable and Continuing Education
edited by Richard Adler
and Walter S. Baer

ASPEN NOTEBOOK ON GOVERNMENT AND THE MEDIA
edited ty William L. Rivers
and Michael J. Nyhan

THE ELECTRONIC BOX OFFICE: Humanities and Arts on the Cable
edited by Richard Adler
and Walter S. Baer

*FREEDOM OF THE PRESS VS. PUBLIC ACCESS
Benno C. Schmidt, Jr.

GETTING TO SESAME STREET: Origins of the Children's Television Workshop
Richard M Polsky

TELEVISION AS A SOCIAL FORCE
edited by Douglass Cater
and Richard Adler

Also published by Praeger:

CHILDREN'S TELEVISION: An Analysis of Weekend and After School Programming
F. Earle Barcus

*THE MEDIA AND THE LAW
edited by Howard Simons
and Joseph A. Califano, Jr.

TELEVISION IN THE CORPORATE INTEREST
Richard Bunce

*Also available in paper as a PSS Student Edition.